To Esther

Enjoy!

Paul

NOT GOING BACK

NOT GOING BACK

How to Lead
Into The New Future

PAUL BLUM

LIONCREST
PUBLISHING

Hardcover ISBN: 978-1-5445-2933-2
Paperback ISBN: 978-1-5445-2934-9
Ebook ISBN: 978-1-5445-2935-6

To my wife, Lauren,
co-founding partner of Lucky 5 and the love of my life.

Contents

Foreword

—Pam Allyn,
December 2021

*T**his book will change your life.*
As an entrepreneur, I have spent, as perhaps you have, too, many dutiful hours engaged in the habit of reading leadership books, business books, and lifestyle books, searching for the words and inspiration that would guide me and coach me to a clarity of understanding of my own sense of my leadership style in the workplace. *How can I best support my teams? How can I best do the work that will become my legacy?*

None of these other books ever matched the benefits I received from the yearslong conversations I've had with Paul himself. I'd read these books, listen to podcasts, search for memorable quotes, and then come right back to my "Ask Paul" notes. I have been lucky enough to have Paul coach and lead me in my own business practices, my leadership journey in founding my own businesses, working as a senior executive at a public company, and creating a startup. I'd save up questions to ask him, questions I'd have about vision setting, enactment of goals, the problems and challenges of daily life as an executive or as a founder, and revenue-generating ideas to practice. I'd take away from our meetings seminal insights on life, well-being, ambitious thinking and action, and deep knowledge and understanding of business at every level, from the small startup to the large corporation, which provided me with the clarity I couldn't find in quite the same way anywhere else. My teams have often said we should make a T-shirt that says, "Paul says..." because these are the seminal insights that have guided us to create and build our programs and companies.

Now, in this past year, in the creation of my new venture, Dewey, a parent learning platform, I have gotten to see afresh the genius of Paul: the way he takes very complex ideas and simplifies them, the way he makes it possible for each and every one of us to take the next steps necessary for growth and success. The work he does helps leaders develop success in and for their companies. I have tried to identify what the genius is in what Paul does that is simply unlike any other leadership guidance I have ever received. At the heart of this guidance is his singular, brilliant, exceptional understanding of human nature and the world we live in. He has a dual understanding of the way times demand certain responses around marketing and sales, all the operational elements necessary for today's world, and why now is different from even the recent past. But the second part of his understanding is what motivates and inspires an individual to do their best, be their best, and go beyond what they even imagined possible. His innate understanding of what drives people to succeed, what will motivate them, combined with a sensitivity to emotion, gives us all a way to see every problem as an opportunity and every person filled with potential to do their best, and beyond their best.

Here in this extraordinary book, we all have access to Paul's brilliant thinking and guidance, encapsulated for us to use as a road map for our—your—life's work. It is a humane, compassionate, fearless approach to business, leadership, and life. Now you, too, can benefit from the profound wisdom of "Paul says..." Now you, too, will have a road map for your own creative business leadership. A road map for how to lead in a way that models lifelong learning, and a deeply positive, optimistic, energized, self-reflective growth journey that is as much for you as it is for the health and well-being of your business, and the idea that is taking root inside you, moving it forward powerfully into the world.

Paul Blum's career is a powerful testimony to the power of one person to shape an entire industry with one seminal idea: he starts with the creative genius, the brilliance of the human spirit, the way what we have inside of us is what builds an entire ecosystem, a new idea, a transformational solution. His résumé is spectacular regarding this, and yet, he never introduces himself that way. He'll say at the outset of a meeting, "I help people." Paul served as CEO of Kenneth Cole and David Yurman, in each case celebrating the strength and power of the companies' founders, while at the same time building operational excellence so their visions could flourish. His leadership at Juicy Couture and Henri Bendel further crystallized his impact on the fashion industry in how he foresaw trends, always ten steps ahead of what was coming, while still being able to center what felt and feels lasting in what people want and hunger for. In more recent years, he has brought his unique brand of genius to the startup world: the understanding he has of marketing and sales, of operations, of what it takes for a day-to-day leader to translate their vision into reality. Paul has a wide network of true fans, all of us who have been transformed by the journey with him. We want you to have it too. And now you can.

In this book, Paul speaks to these fast-changing times as only he can do: with a fresh eye and a deeply innovative approach. He speaks powerfully about the "people priority" in the work we do as leaders: how to create work environments that will retain and sustain our employees so that they are happy, motivated, and motivational. He helps us move away from superficial marketing approaches to a far deeper strategy built around the needs of customers, with eye-opening insights into how we meet and define their needs. Paul's guidance leads us to consider how we build a sustaining, inclusive culture that is focused on our values. His step-by-step process gets us there.

The writing and ideas, so timely for the how of now, so timeless for the work of always, are clear of mind and spirit, guiding without being pedantic, wise without being exclusive, compassionate while at the same time deeply rigorous in thought and action. This book is truly and stupendously good. It is so helpful, and so memorable. Paul's brilliant, accessible voice is right there with us: approachable, patient, caring, dynamic, and exciting.

As Paul says, you've got this. Whatever the dream is that brought you to open this book and begin here, that dream is well worth planning, strategizing, executing.

This book will change your life.

Introduction

I was recently asked to present at a global retail industry summit. Like so many conferences in our new, postpandemic world, this gathering was online, and all meetings and presentations were held over Zoom. This is how things are now. I'm sure we will eventually be working in a hybrid environment: a mix of dynamic, in-person events amplified by digital technology. Some people will be physically present and some remote. It's a new world, and it's not going back to the way it used to be. How we work has been permanently altered.

With so many people starting new jobs, taking on new roles, and even developing their own businesses remotely, these types of events are pretty frequent. People working from home or in shared workspaces need advice on how work really *works* in this new environment.

They're also looking for human connection.

The subject of this particular presentation was supposed to be "digital brand marketing strategy." As a highly adapted introvert, I was dreading it. I don't like giving speeches, even when it's just to a screen with my own face on it. I was also squirming at having to sit through the long, embarrassing introduction that the moderator was about to deliver. I know it's their job to talk about my past accomplishments as a CEO and compliment me on my thriving consulting practice, but it makes me terribly uncomfortable.

What I *really* wanted to do was skip to the Q and A portion of the presentation as quickly as possible. Does anyone really care about my résumé? I don't think so. I believe what people want is to have someone listen to their issues and help them find solutions. They don't want to hear another word from our sponsors.

They want answers.

This book is my way to share the answers to people's most pressing questions about leadership in our fast-changing, challenging, and stressful times. Most of these questions are not about technical business issues at all—that "digital brand marketing strategy" talk was full of people who were thinking about far deeper issues than internet advertising.

No, most of the big questions people have about their work are about *people*: how they can inspire them, attract them, engage them, and partner with them. Getting the answers to these questions, and developing the skills required to use those answers, is incredibly important. Without this foundation, none of the technical business issues will matter much.

I learned this as a CEO, and I see it every day in my advisory practice. Happy, productive, engaged people do better work. They are more creative and connect with customers better. If you need more convincing of this, I suggest reading the work of Zeynep Ton, an MIT professor who uses in-depth case studies to prove that smart investment in people has a direct return on investment for the brand and for the financial health of the company.[1]

This "people priority" is especially important today, in a world in which the consumer is incredibly empowered by the internet to make choices about and transact with brands whose values they share and whose work community reflects their own culture. No amount of superficial marketing will change that. And it's not going back.

---

1   Zeynep Ton, *The Good Jobs Strategy: How the Smartest Companies Invest in Employees to Lower Costs and Boost Profits* (New York: New Harvest, 2014).

Your work needs to be authentic, and great leaders are the lynchpin in creating this healthy, vibrant system.

Creating the New Future

Just how does a system that prioritizes people work? I like to use this flowchart to help visualize it:

FUTURE CYCLE

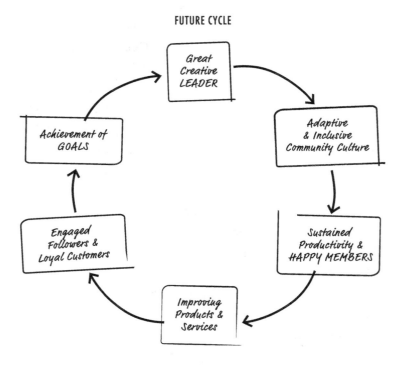

Great leaders with strong values create an engaged, diverse community, which in turn creates great jobs. Because people are happier in good jobs where they can be themselves, they do better work, which in turn leads to happier customers—and *that* leads to great financial results.

The purpose of this book is to answer the key questions that get at the heart of how leaders can harness the power of this cycle to accomplish their own goals. These key questions are:

- Why is self-awareness so important, and how can you achieve it?

- Why are values important, and how can you clearly define them?

- How can you intentionally design a culture?

- How do you develop a more inclusive community?

- How can an organization adapt to change while staying focused on its mission?

- How can we sustain ourselves, our community, and our planet as we grow?

When these touchstone questions guide your thinking, you'll begin to approach your challenges with the mindset of a great leader. This book will help develop the skills needed to ask better questions and work in partnership with your community to find the answers—or create them from scratch when you need to.

However, this book is *not* a quick-fix manual that proposes to predict or describe the "new normal."

I realize that many people are looking for a buzzword that will explain how to succeed in a postpandemic business environment. And while much of my career in the fashion industry was spent reading the tea leaves to successfully predict trends, this book is not about fads.

Gimmicks are a waste of time, and there's no substitute for the deep work of understanding yourself as a leader and connecting with your community on a personal level. There's no quick fix here.

Instead, this book is about gaining self-awareness. It's about taking the first step on what will be a journey of lifelong listening and learning. It's about developing the timeless skills that will help you adapt to the ever-developing future. It's about recognizing and embracing change instead of fighting to stay in the past.

The future is here, and just when you think you understand it, it's gone—morphing into something else entirely. Get used to this, because it's not going back.

How to Use This Book

First, a note about the language of this book. You'll notice the words I choose are a little different. For example, I rarely refer to people as *employees*. Instead, I use more specific language like *partner*, *member*, or *role player*. In doing this, I aim to be as specific as possible about what a person brings to the table, rather than just focusing on their status as a subordinate.

I also don't refer to groups as *companies* or *teams*, but rather as a *community*. This is more inclusive of the many types of communities who need great leadership, whether the work they do is for profit or for the greater good. It also brings the focus squarely onto our shared humanity, which is an important shift that today's successful leaders must embrace.

Second, in this book I tell several stories to illustrate lessons and ideas. These stories are mostly composites and not necessarily about one person or organization. Names have been changed to protect people's privacy.

Finally, a word about how you can get the most out of this book. You can, of course, choose to read straight through to get an overview of the process of developing critical leadership skills. I've arranged each session in such a way that they build on each other, so earlier lessons prepare you for later conversations and problem solving. You can read this book from cover to cover and complete the exercises at the end of each session.

However, you can also focus on a specific session to address your most urgent needs. This book is all about answering your questions, so feel free to focus on any session you feel is needed, at anytime you need the support. The work of leadership is ongoing, and you may need to readdress and sharpen different skills at different times.

My main recommendation is that you do *not* skip Session 1: Showing Up, because putting yourself into the process is critical.

Finally, I love feedback. Please don't hesitate to contact me with questions or comments as you engage in this important work. You can reach out anytime by emailing me at paul@ notgoingback.net.

Session 1

SHOWING UP

Create Your
Leadership Mindset

We live in a fast-changing world where technology and major global events have accelerated the pace of change in our lives, both at work and at home. Because of this, some of us haven't had time to adjust to new ways of working and communicating. Until now, we've been muddling through waters that are churning with change—some of us floating along, others struggling mightily to keep our heads above water.

For over one hundred years, the Industrial Revolution has promised that all progress comes in the form of a new invention, and in that time, people have learned to structure their work like a well-oiled machine. This is particularly true of business hierarchies in the post-World War II era. It's easy to think that, with all of our reliance on computers and the internet, human skills don't matter as much: technology will solve everything eventually, and if you just find the right solution, your problems will disappear.

But this type of thinking—namely, that strict hierarchical organization and technical solutions are central to success—is grossly outdated. With the technological floodgates fully open, old hierarchies and expectations are just too slow to adapt to the pace of change. Steering your ship through the raging, rising seas of change is going to require a completely different mindset.

The truth is that our technology-accelerated world is still driven by *people*, both individually and in communities. Whether you're leading a team, a company, or an entire corporation, people are still at the core of your work. This is your community, and it is first and foremost a human one.

In fact, I would argue that social skills matter even more today than they ever did. After all, social media and the new transparency that it provides into businesses and brands means that we are now all public figures. Everything you do in your company is—or will eventually be—visible to the public. Your business culture is showing, whether you intend it to or not.

As a leader, you are on display, both to your team and to the world at large. Your personal qualities will drive your community to success and lay the foundation for a business culture that reflects your true values.

But before you can effectively lead others, you must make sure that you are, in your heart, prepared to show up. This work begins with your own mindset. This is what it means to show up: you are ready and willing to look inward first, to lay a personal foundation that will support all of the leadership skills you'll learn in future sessions.

Our work in this session will focus on three key outcomes: a **sustainable mindset** that allows you to maintain boundaries and balance in your work, an **attitude of** curiosity that allows you to experiment and learn as you journey toward increased self-awareness, and a **clarification of the values** that drive everything you do.

By the way, you don't have to be born with the scientific method memorized to engage in experimentation, and you don't have to be a Zen master to achieve balance. Both of these ways of looking at the world are eminently learnable. Consider this session your invitation to begin developing the leadership mindset that will form the foundation of all of your work moving forward.

The Architecture: A Sustainable Mindset

For anyone who seeks to effectively lead a community, a sustainable mindset is the foundation upon which all other skills will be built.

Notice first, however, that your mindset isn't a skill. It's more fundamental than that, because your mindset gets at the heart of who you are as a person. It's how you interpret situations, how you interact with others, and how you respond to problems, adversity, and endless change. Your mindset is a big part of who you really are, as a leader and as a person.

A *sustainable* mindset is one that allows you to set boundaries, achieve balance, and feel comfortable with experimentation. It also allows you to operate from a position of openness, as you accept that you will learn from both success and failure and that your abilities can be strengthened by practice. A sustainable mindset is the opposite of perfectionism and instead provides fertile ground in your mind to learn, grow, and change.

It's important to note that we aren't all born with a sustainable mindset—and even if we were, the world around us does a lot to change it and make us more rigid.

Throughout your life, you have probably become far more rigid than you were as a child, and that's understandable—the stakes get higher as you grow into adulthood, especially as you take on increasing tasks and responsibilities as a leader.

I like to think of a sustainable mindset as the architecture that allows leaders to build successful organizations. Architects pay close attention to the strength of the foundation as they design their buildings, and that foundation must be both strong enough to support the structure and flexible enough to bend rather than break when buffeted by external forces. A sustainable mindset provides just this type of foundation for your work as a leader—and you can learn to adjust your thinking with practice.

Mindset Development Workflow

This workflow focuses on three main elements of a sustainable mindset and provides practical suggestions for you to begin to work in a way that honors your own needs as a human being—and eventually makes space for you to honor your team's needs as well.

Step One: Understand the Drawbacks of Technology

Technology enables you to work twenty-four hours a day, seven days a week, 365 days a year. But that is not sustainable. You're going to burn out if you work all the time.

On the surface, this is an obvious statement. But the pressure created by technology's ability to be "always on" has led people to feel the need to keep up with an impossibly relentless pace. Email pings at all hours, video conferencing in our private spaces, internet that lets you turn any corner of your home or car into an office: these are all wonderfully useful advancements, but they've also completely invaded our lives. The tools that made it possible for many businesses to survive the pandemic are the very same tools that are pushing you to work at all hours of the day.

You simply cannot do this forever. You need space away from work, and in today's world, that means putting some limits on how you—and your community—interact with technology.

For example, I once consulted on a project for a company where the CEO would routinely send emails to his team at all hours of the night. Whenever he got an idea, he jotted it down and sent it off so that he wouldn't forget about it. This CEO had no expectation that anyone actually *answered* those emails in the middle of the night, and he was perfectly content that recipients would see them and respond in the morning.

But the people who were on the receiving end of midnight and 3:00 a.m. emails were distressed. They were well aware of the time stamps on these emails, which made them feel like they were slacking off—even though they were off the clock and perfectly justified in getting a good night's sleep! But that didn't matter. His late-night emails insidiously created a culture that encouraged people to be "always on"—and it was incredibly damaging to morale.

There are a couple things at play here. First, many apps, platforms, and messaging programs are designed to be addictive. All those red alert buttons and sounds demand your attention, and they act a bit like a slot machine, rewarding your brain every time they go off. Even if you don't want to be tied to your email at home, there's a part of your brain that's always scanning the horizon for the next message.

Second, many organizations are structured with a hierarchical and/or competitive structure, which makes saying no to a "superior" incredibly difficult—your job could be on the line. And even if your manager is understanding, there's always the fear that someone else is working harder than you. The pressure to keep up is enormous, *even if that pressure was never intentionally placed.*

Remember: You *cannot* work all of the time, even though you have the tools to do so. You will burn out.

Fortunately, there are some easy ways to keep technology functioning as a propeller rather than an anchor.

A low-tech solution for keeping email more manageable is to keep a notebook to jot down ideas as you have them, then bundle them into a single daily or weekly email to keep things more efficient. This will also model healthy technology use for your community and keep the pressure to respond at a minimum.

For a high-tech solution, consider an advanced email program that allows you to schedule your emails. You can set up a rule that no emails go out during nonbusiness hours so your computer will simply hold them until the clock strikes nine (or whenever your day begins).

Step Two: Create and Communicate Boundaries

Modern communication technology is here to stay, and that's a good thing: we need it to function! But we also need to draw healthy boundaries around work in this new age. Boundaries are an essential part of a sustainable mindset.

Because it's now *possible* to work at all hours, you need to decide when you are working and when you are not. You also need to let others know when you are available and when you are not. This includes your work community and your home community, so that people know what to expect from you. For instance, if you are clear with everyone in your life that you are done working at 6:00 p.m., your colleagues know not to expect a reply to an email until morning, and your family knows that they have your full attention at the dinner table.

It's also important that *you* know when you're working and when you're not. To that end, I'd like to share some best practices that you should strive to master as you develop your work-life boundaries.

Boundary Best Practices

- **Clarify Responsibilities:** What is your responsibility, and what is not? It is perfectly okay to step up and say that something is outside of your zone of responsibility. We often feel pressure to take on everything, whether due to a sense of perfectionism, obligation, or even enthusiasm. But getting clear on who is responsible for what isn't just good for you—it's also a kindness to everyone around you.

- **Normalize Boundaries:** As a leader, you set the tone for your community, so seize the opportunity to model boundaries. As you inform your team of your boundaries, invite them to do the same—then scrupulously honor those boundaries. Too often, leaders stigmatize boundaries by creating a culture that valorizes constant work. It doesn't have to be that way, and it all starts with you.

- **Be Human:** Having boundaries doesn't make you selfish, it makes you generous—to yourself and to everyone around you. As you discuss your boundaries, try opening up about why they're important to you and how you benefit as a person from having some downtime just to be yourself. If you're not in the habit of creating boundaries around your work, start by jotting down three to five things that are important enough to you to make time for in your life, and use that note to remind you to close your laptop when your day is done.

- **Develop Other Interests:** If you struggled to fill a sticky note with activities you enjoy, it's time to develop some hobbies. Activities outside of work—spending time with family and friends, art, exercise, education, and reading—will help provide a fresh perspective by giving you a break from work. The rest will actually help increase your productivity and problem-solving abilities.

Step Three: Develop a Practice

Finally, there are times when even the best boundaries are difficult to maintain, and your home life may not provide the respite you need from your work life. It isn't enough simply to have hobbies, either, because these activities are optional—they can be easily brushed aside when things get busy.

That's why it's so important to find time in your day for a practice. When we talk about a practice, most people will first think of meditation, yoga, or some other spiritual practice designed to refresh and renew. These are excellent choices, but I prefer a broader definition. For our purposes, a practice is something that you do by yourself in a quiet space. It's an activity that you do in order to get better at it, but you're not after perfection.

You're embracing it for the sheer joy of doing it. There are no goals in a practice other than regular, daily engagement.

A meaningful practice requires just three things:

- A dedicated time period each day

- Uninterrupted quiet time

- An activity you enjoy that you want to get better at

A practice focuses on the process, not the product. It's a sacred time and space for you to just be yourself for a time and embrace what it means to be a lifelong learner. When you develop a practice, you remind yourself that all skills are learnable—especially when you keep at them.

One of the biggest benefits of cultivating a practice is that it gives you time to approach things with a beginner's mind. When you are learning something, everything is, at first, an experiment. This mindset shifts your focus to improving a little bit each time, rather than worrying about specific outcomes or an arbitrary definition of success.

In other words, it's often the opposite of how we approach our working life. A practice forgives you for mistakes and offers you room to grow. It provides not just respite, but restoration.

I want to be clear here that I'm not suggesting developing a practice as a "life hack" or some type of shortcut to turbocharge your performance. My idea of a practice is an antidote to the grind, a time to spend on yourself to appreciate the journey.

Personally, I choose early morning exercise as my practice. I make time in my day, every day, to do an exercise routine, and it has made a huge difference in my life. I feel better each time I do it: a little stronger, a little faster, a little healthier. There's no goal to run the New York City Marathon or lose twenty pounds before Thanksgiving. It's just practice.

That's not to say that you have to embrace an early-morning wake-up call to hit the gym. Your practice can be anything that brings you joy and allows you time to focus on getting better at something that has nothing to do with work. If you don't currently have a practice, you may have to experiment until you find one that you enjoy, but the benefits are well worth it.

Ideas for Your Personal Practice

- Running
- Walking
- Solo sports: swimming, rock climbing, figure skating, archery, etc.
- Yoga
- Meditation
- Puzzles: crosswords, sudoku, jigsaws, etc.
- Music: playing an instrument, singing, listening to albums, etc.
- Reading
- Writing: poetry, stories, journaling, etc.
- Arts: drawing, painting, ceramics, photography, etc.
- Nature activities: gardening, hiking, fishing, etc.

Putting It All Together

Our lives today are packed to the gills with so many things: technology, performance, media, work—the list goes on and on. For most of us, technology has entered our lives and filled it with so much *stuff* that we've lost our practice space. We've let go of quiet time to read or just sit still and think.

Cultivating a sustainable mindset is all about getting that time back. It requires putting technology in its place, setting and maintaining clear boundaries around work, and creating a dedicated practice period to recharge. This method will allow you to develop into a strong leader with a fertile mind and the ability to approach your work with sustainable energy. It's the key to everything that follows.

The Engine: An Attitude of Curiosity

If a sustainable mindset is the architecture that provides structure for the rest of your work as a leader, an attitude of curiosity is the engine that will allow you to press forward with new ideas and solutions as you grow. Curiosity is the key to flexibility, the attitude that will keep you from stagnating in "the way we've always done things." Curiosity keeps you moving in whatever direction you need to—even if it wasn't part of your original plan.

Like a sustainable mindset, an attitude of curiosity isn't necessarily preprogrammed. You can learn to approach the world with curiosity, even if you haven't done much of that type of thinking since childhood. Working with curiosity means asking the right questions, then listening to the answers with honest attention and an open mind. This is a critical element of developing your skills as a leader, because the first step to working with others is understanding yourself. And to do that, you need to begin by asking questions.

Curiosity Development Workflow

This workflow provides specific guidance on how to develop and harness an attitude of curiosity that will lead to greater self-awareness. It's not quite enough to be curious in general; instead, you need to be able to turn the process inward to discover who you are as a person. Before you can tackle any additional skills, you need to know yourself, your strengths, and your needs.

Step One: Ask Yourself Five Big Questions

It's time to get curious about who you are as a person, right now. To do this, I want you to ask yourself five important questions following what I like to call the **Question Progression**. This basic series of questions will help you get to the heart of any issue to figure out what's essential, and we will discuss the Question Progression in greater detail in Session 4. For this session, we're turning the questions inward to focus on the self.

Take the time to think deeply about these questions and answer them thoroughly. If you'd like a printable worksheet to help you gather your thoughts, you can download a PDF at www.notgoingback.net. Otherwise, you can write your answers in a notebook or journal.

THE QUESTION PROGRESSION: FOCUS ON THE SELF

1. **Who?** Who are you right now, at this point in your life?

2. **What?** What are your goals and aspirations?

3. **Why?** Why do you do what you do? Why are you dedicated to and engaged with your work?

4. **How?** How do you want to achieve your goals? What methods do you want to embrace?

5. **When?** When do you want to achieve your goals?
   Is your timeline long term, or is this something you want to do right away?

Note that you may find it helpful to focus on a single goal at a time and repeat the Question Progression for each of your most important goals.

Step Two: Listen to Your Answers

It's not enough just to ask the right questions. You also have to dig deep and listen to the answers. Listening is a crucial leadership skill that we tackle more thoroughly in Session 3, but for now, we can begin with some of the basics of good listening as you turn inward to apply them to yourself:

- **Don't multitask.** Limit distractions as you consider your answers to the questions above. Then, as you go back and read what you have written, ensure that you devote your full attention to your words. You deserve your full focus, so provide it.

- **Don't rush to judgment.** Try to avoid a knee-jerk reaction to your answers, both as you write them and as you reread them. It may help to come back to them after a day or two to provide some space to reflect. If it helps silence your inner critic, pretend that a colleague wrote them and give them your patience.

- **Think quietly.** Once you've reread your answers, take time to consider your words. Are they accurate? Are they honest? What are you telling yourself here? Give yourself time to consider what they mean and the many options you have to address them.

Step Three: Deepen Your Self-Awareness with a Trusted Partner

Now that you've gotten curious about who you are and what you want to achieve, it's time to take that work to the next level. In this exercise, you'll work with a partner to assess how well you know yourself. Does the way you see yourself match up with how others see you? This is critical information to gather as you consider what skills you most need to develop to move forward successfully.

You will need to work with a trusted partner—someone who knows you well, especially when it comes to your work. This could be a business partner, close coworker, or mentor. You will each answer the six questions below to rate different aspects of your current mindset. In addition to a number rating, you and your partner should also provide a brief explanation of your thinking.

Note that you are both answering these questions about *you*, at the same time, without discussing your responses—yet. You can always repeat the exercise later to dig into your partner's mindset if they're interested. Download and print out as many copies of the PDF worksheet as you like at www.notgoingback.net.

THE SELF-AWARENESS ASSESSMENT

1. Do you see the best in people?

1	2	3	4	5
Never	Rarely	Sometimes	Often	Always

   Explain:

2. Are you optimistic about new projects?

1	2	3	4	5
Never	Rarely	Sometimes	Often	Always

   Explain:

3. Do you inspire others to feel good about their work?

1	2	3	4	5
Never	Rarely	Sometimes	Often	Always

   Explain:

4. Are you a good listener who is open to new ideas, even if they contradict your original thinking?

1	2	3	4	5
Never	Rarely	Sometimes	Often	Always

   Explain:

5. Are you able to focus on the project at hand without jumping around?

1	2	3	4	5
Never	Rarely	Sometimes	Often	Always

   Explain:

6. Are you a good delegator who both helps others and accepts help from them?

1	2	3	4	5
Never	Rarely	Sometimes	Often	Always

   Explain:

Writing your answers down is an important step! If you don't write them down, you will be tempted to change your answers when you hear your partner's thoughts.

Once you are both done writing, discuss your answers together. In what ways do you see yourself accurately, and in what ways do an outside observer's opinions differ from your own? This can be an eye-opening exercise.

You might not always like what you hear. For example, if you see yourself as a good listener and your partner has given you a low score, hear them out. They are here to help you, and the only way you can improve is to embrace the truth and get working on that part of yourself.

If you're interested in scoring this like a quiz, you'll want to take your partner's rating and subtract it from yours on each question (ignore negative signs—they don't matter). A 0 is perfect—you were in agreement about your skills, which means you have excellent self-awareness. A 4 is a big difference, and this indicates that in this particular area, you aren't very self-aware. That's an indication that you need to develop these skills—which we will do throughout the rest of this book.

The Culmination: Your Values

Now that you've completed your first round of self-awareness work, it's time to put your sustainable mindset and active curiosity to work to explore your personal values. Your **values** are your unshakeable beliefs. They are what are most important to you, both in your life and your work. Your values are the principles you live by that will never change, no matter how the circumstances around you evolve.

Many people struggle with putting their values into words. They *feel* them—often deeply—but have not taken the time to articulate them. Most people in positions of leadership spend their time completing tasks and solving problems to make sure that day-to-day operations run smoothly. This is important, of course, but the deeper work of leadership requires you to know your values as a human being *before* you can use them to guide your community. This is a critical starting point to the type of leadership that will see you through today's swift currents of change.

We will discuss the importance of values throughout this book, focusing particularly on issues of transparency and culture in future sessions. For now, it's enough to note that your personal values will be on full display in your organization— and to the world at large, thanks to the internet and social media. For this reason, it's important to be clear about your values from the outset.

So let's begin this critical work. Consider your answers to the questions below, and keep your work handy to refer to as you work through the remaining sessions in the book.

THE VALUES BRAINSTORM

1. List the values that are most important to you. What matters to you as a human being? What do you want to bring to the world? What traits do you value in yourself and others? What is your purpose? These are big questions, but there are no right or wrong answers. Just list all the values that come to mind for now.

2. Now, review your list. What themes do you see in your answers? Can some of your ideas be combined into a single word or phrase? See if you can streamline your ideas by turning them into single words that encapsulate the essence of your thoughts. (For example: honesty, creativity, kindness, etc.)

3. Finally, take a look at your list of values above. Which are most important to you? Consider your priorities and list your top one to three values below.

4. Why are these values at the top of your list?

Next Steps

If you've gone through the assessments and exercises in this session, you've already taken a big step forward in developing a more sustainable mindset for leadership. If your self-awareness scores didn't provide any major red flags, you are well prepared with the self-knowledge it takes to lead. You can continue to Session 2 to dive into more specific skills.

If you have concerns, you may wish to seek out some additional coaching to develop better awareness of your strengths and weaknesses. Gaining a thorough knowledge of yourself is key, and it's well worth doing some personal development work first if you're struggling with your basic mindset and self-awareness. For specific resources, see the Appendix.

No matter where you are in your self-awareness journey, continue to create boundaries by deciding how and when you will work—and be sure to let your community know! Finally, find yourself some time in your day to start your personal practice tomorrow. No matter what you choose to devote your time to, spending time in beginner's mind will help you approach the rest of your work in this book with curiosity and openness.

DESIGNING YOUR COMMUNITY

Get Intentional About Building Your Team

Now that you've begun the important work of developing your self-awareness, it's time to begin to identify and attract other people to work with you on your goals. In the past, a work community tended to develop over time. Here's how it worked:

1. An individual identifies a need and comes up with a great idea for a product to solve that problem.

2. That individual finds someone who agrees with them and shares their vision for developing the product.

3. The pair then finds a third person who knows how to sell that product.

4. The trio brings on someone to financially manage the company so they can focus on the product.

5. The small organization begins selling the product, and as demand grows, they bring on additional people to fill roles in an ad hoc way.

This is a classic model of how a small company gets bigger. The focus here is on doing whatever it takes to bring a product to market, and this is understandable. But it's also a fairly haphazard way to develop a community because the sole focus is on putting out fires—that is, bringing people on to perform specific tasks as needed, without much attention to their values or how they might contribute to the overall culture of the organization and community at large.

One thing you will notice, in this book and in your work, is that *the old way of doing things no longer works, and it's not going back!* The old way of designing a community without much thought to how it would function as a cohesive unit has led to many people feeling unheard and unhappy—a recipe for low morale and poor outcomes in any group.

Now that you have developed a stronger sense of your personal strengths and values from your work in Session 1, it's time to apply those values to intentionally design your community. The earlier you can do this, the stronger your community will be. It's incredibly difficult to reverse engineer a strong culture, so this session focuses on the identification of key community members and the systems of communication you will use to tie this group together.

A Story: The Old Boys Club

Back in 2019, I flew to Chicago to consult with a client on a retail project. His company was a clothing retailer with twenty stores throughout the Midwest, but no online business to speak of. The CEO hired my consulting organization to help develop their fledgling online business so they could expand into internet sales.

When I sat down with the CEO in his office, the first thing he did was put his devices on the polished walnut desk in front of me. "This one," he said, pointing to an iPhone, "is for taking pictures of my kids so I can share them with the grandparents."

Then he pointed to a scuffed-up Blackberry from 1991. "And that one is for work."

He sat back in his chair and looked at me. "That's all I've got for technology."

This CEO clearly didn't think much of modern communication technology, and therein laid the initial challenge of this project: bringing an old-fashioned brick-and-mortar retailer into the twenty-first century to help them grow their business and capture online market share.

But then I met with the team.

Every time I work with a new client, I begin with an assessment of their business overall. This assessment always starts with meeting the leadership team in the organization and figuring out what makes them tick. Before I can diagnose issues or begin to suggest a solution, I need to know what makes a group tick. Understanding the community they've built is a crucial part of developing goals and plans.

So I met with the leaders of several departments: finance, sales, and product development. When they assembled in one room, it was clear that they had all been working together for some time. They were all older white men living in and around Chicago. They all spoke the same language, the type of verbal shorthand that develops in a group over many years. They even finished each other's sentences when I asked them about the business.

To a man, this group was pretty happy with their business already. They didn't understand why they needed to devote time and effort to the online portion of their business, since things were going well enough, as they had been for many years. In fact, none of these men actually knew very much about the online portion of their business at all.

That's because their e-commerce business was run by a young woman who worked in the Chicago office but wasn't a part of the management team. Her job title? Assistant IT Director.

Let that sink in for a moment. This company was running e-commerce as a division of their Information Systems department—not sales or even technology, but basic computing and troubleshooting for staff.

Right away, I could see several problems in this organization that were keeping them from reaching their goal of a successful e-commerce launch:

- The company's leadership did not fully understand or value the technologically driven world we live in. This attitude came from the top.

- The leadership team was well aligned, but that came with significant blind spots about their diverse clientele's needs and expectations.

- The leadership team had also created an echo chamber for themselves, so they rarely heard different ideas or had their assumptions questioned.

- The leadership team did not include the young woman who was actually in charge of running the department they aimed to create, and her expertise was not fully utilized or even recognized.

Intentional Leadership

This story highlights the truth that the old way of building a community is no longer sufficient to meet the moment we live in—that is, one of rapid technological and cultural change.

When the men in that Midwestern company built their community, they did so in the traditional way, with their eyes on the prize of selling clothing. People were added to the community over time because of their expertise in various areas (sales, marketing, logistics) rather than with an eye toward how they would function together as a culture. Over time, their habits of communication solidified, so they were completely unprepared to include a valuable new community member—a woman—who was different in her background and thinking. Their communication systems actually excluded the expertise they needed, and they *weren't even aware* of the deficit.

Intentionality—in building community and communicating with each member—is key to leading a group to successful outcomes.

Too often, discussions of leadership ignore the fundamental skill of intentionality in favor of technical solutions to specific problems. But the truth is that we have no way of knowing what specific problems will pop up in the future. Did anyone see a global pandemic and economic shutdown coming? It's impossible to prepare for every eventuality, but you can prepare your community to respond to whatever the world has in store for you. The key skill is *intentionality*, which will allow you to build your community into one that is as resilient as possible.

To help focus your intention, this session focuses on two key competencies every leader must develop to create and guide a successful community. The first is identifying key community members and determining the role they will play within the group. The second is choosing the systems and technologies to openly communicate within that community.

Community Development Workflow

The success of any endeavor depends on the resilience of the community members who come together around your mission. Before you can lead a community, you must identify the people you need—and want—to work with. This workflow will help you understand the different roles people play in your community so you have appropriate expectations of their contributions and can work with them in the most effective way.

Step One: Who Are Your People?

In the old way of doing things, bosses hired people based purely on the particular skill they needed at the moment. But in a world where constant change requires people to pivot in their jobs to take on new—and as yet unimagined—responsibilities, it now makes more sense to consider the *role* your community members play in the big picture rather than just taking a snapshot of their current function.

So what, exactly, are these roles? I break them into four main groups: supporters, mentors, partners, and role players.

SUPPORTERS

Supporters are friends and family who care deeply about you. They're always on your side, and they want what's best for you. It's important to include these people and take their counsel because they know you best. For this reason, you may find that your supporters are one of your greatest resources in developing some of the self-awareness skills we discussed in the previous session. Because we now live in a world where the line between work and personal life is blurred, supporters may play a larger role than ever before when it comes to your mission. They're more likely than ever to serve as a sounding board for your concerns, help provide extra hands when you're in startup mode, and even provide material support or investment in the beginning.

While supporters are a great resource that can keep you buoyed and balanced, there is a line between taking their counsel and taking their advice. Supporters look at everything from your perspective, so their input is likely to be biased toward your happiness rather than your mission's success. They may not have a full picture of your goals, so take what they offer as caring counsel—but don't rely on their specific advice, because they lack experience in the specific areas you're looking to grow into.

MENTORS

Mentors are experts in specific areas of opportunity for your mission. Unlike supporters, mentors are the ones with answers to your questions about the everyday details of running your organization and achieving your goals. You may seek a mentor in your general field for overarching advice, or you may seek out a mentor with more specific skills in an area you feel you need to build upon.

It's important to remember that mentorship is a two-way relationship. As the mentee, you receive guidance and get valuable information to help you move forward. But you are also providing the mentor with an opportunity to give back, which is likely their motivation for engaging in the relationship. Ideally, mentorship is a satisfying, ongoing process for both parties.

PARTNERS

Partners are people with complementary skills and strengths that offset your weaknesses. (If you haven't yet completed Session 1, I encourage you to do so, as it will help you understand your weaknesses and help you determine what you need from your partners.) For example, if you love product development but dislike sales and marketing, your partners should help fill these areas of need. These needs may be skill based, but consider personality strengths and weaknesses as well.

Partners should share your values, but not to the point of mirroring you exactly. You want them to challenge you! Open, honest communication is key, especially when you disagree. Because you'll be spending so much time with your partners, you should genuinely like them and enjoy their company.

Finally, partners should have a stake in the success of your endeavor. A true partner is one with an equity stake in your mission so they share your motivations and will work together with you. A "paid partner" is no partner at all, because they have a safety net that separates them from your financial and emotional investment.

ROLE PLAYERS

Role players are the members of your community that you bring on to fulfill a specific area of need. In the old way of doing things, this meant hiring an employee based on a specific skill that was measured by educational benchmarks and years of experience. In today's world, however, a role player might not be an employee at all. They could be a freelancer or an agency—in fact, you might never work with this role player in person.

When adding role players to your community, it's important to consider their skills, of course, but also their *values*. For example, hiring for honesty, adaptability, and a positive attitude will allow you to develop a community with shared values, which in turn will help you grow into new areas and solve unforeseen problems together. We'll discuss community values in more depth in Session 7, but for now, remember that, when it comes to evaluating a new hire, values and skills matter far more than location, age, education, years of experience, or other résumé background noise.

So who's in your community right now, and who might you need to add in the future? It's time to map your community to get a clearer view of what your working group looks like and how these people function together. To get started, list all of the members of your current community and how they help you achieve your mission.

My Community	Names	Contributions

My
Supporters

My
Mentors

My
Partners

My
Role Players

Take a moment to reflect on your community as it exists right now. What needs are fully met, and what areas could use some strengthening? What people do you need to round out your community and achieve your goals? Create a "wish list" of what that ideal community would look like.

Future Community Members	Role/Title	What They Will Contribute

Future
Supporters

Future
Mentors

Future
Partners

Future
Role Players

Step Two: Hire for Values, Not Just for Skills

The old way of recruiting and hiring meant waiting until you're actively hurting and then seeking a quick solution, typically by creating a detailed job description and spending weeks trying to find a match. But waiting until the need is so great that your goal and your community is suffering forces you into a position of weakness—you're focused on bailing out a sinking ship instead of finding the best way to fix the leak and strengthen the hull.

One of the reasons the old way is so time consuming is that the detailed job description focuses solely on the *functions* of the role player: the day-to-day specifics of the job, technology used, presumed education required, years of experience preferred, and so on. These wish lists are so specific that they tend to lead hirers to consider only people who look just like the people they already work with, leading to the lack of diversity and cultural blind spots highlighted in our opening story.

A better, more intentional way of building your community is with a **candidate-centric approach**. As a leader, you want to create a process by which great talent can be identified and recruited. The balance of power is shifting to workers, and today people are looking for more than just money and benefits when they choose where to work. A candidate-centric approach means figuring out why a candidate should choose *you* and assessing their values in addition to their specific skills.

When you are ready to add to your community, follow the candidate-centric approach to develop a job description and interviewing process.

HIRING WORKSHOP: A CANDIDATE-CENTRIC APPROACH

1. Why would a great candidate take this job?
   Describe both external and internal factors in detail:

External Factors	Internal Factors
Salary:	Flexibility:
Benefits:	Work-Life Balance:
Title:	Community Culture:
Equity:	Personal Growth/Learning:
Fit:	Impact on the World:

2. What can you do to make sure that both external and internal factors are addressed for the candidate?

3. What are you looking for in the ideal candidate?
   Describe both specific skills and character traits that will help them fit into your community—not just as it exists today, but as you wish it to be in the future. (I've added some examples to get you started, but you should feel free to eliminate and add as needed.)

Skills	Character Traits
• Communication	• Curiosity • Motivation
• Technical proficiency	• Transparency • Adaptability
• Conflict resolution • Listening	

4. Develop interview questions that assess these skills and character traits. Brainstorm your ideas below, making sure that each skill and trait is addressed in at least one question.

5. Identify your top three skills and traits above. Then, develop test projects or interview activities to assess how a candidate applies them to a real-life situation. Brainstorm your ideas below.

Take the time to think deeply about your ideal candidate's values with the help of your community. If you'd like a printable worksheet to help you gather your thoughts or develop a more intentional hiring process with your partners, you can download a PDF at www.notgoingback.net.

Step Three: Design Your Communication Systems

Now that you've identified your current community and have developed ways to add new members in an intentional way, it's important to remember that community is a process. It's not a permanent structure. People, especially role players, will move in and out of your community, and that's okay.

This fluidity is natural and even beneficial, but it requires a strong system of communication to keep your community functioning as members come and go. You can't let community wisdom disappear when someone leaves, and you must support new members by making sure they have access to all of the systems and information they need to perform their roles.

Collaboration is crucial in this fast-changing world because you will need to work together efficiently and effectively respond to change when circumstances demand it. Technology provides instant communication, but it can't create transparency and adaptability on its own. It takes an intentional leader to design an effective communication system for their community.

Investing in the design of your communication system will help you share insights, innovate, and solve problems together in real time, which in turn fosters the adaptability required to thrive in today's environment.

There are four basic components to today's communication systems: messaging, video conferencing, data management, and collaboration.

MESSAGING

Email, texts, chat applications, and instant messaging are all ways to communicate between two individuals or in groups. For the purposes of everyday communication, these systems all function in the same way. Which system you choose to use is less important than the rules and processes you set up around their use.

I recommend choosing one system for your community and sticking with it. Using a combination of email, chat rooms, and personal texts creates chaos, and it's far too easy for messages to be lost. Multiple platforms also offer more ways to break down the work-life balance that self-aware leaders seek to maintain— for themselves *and* for their community as a whole.

- We should have our structures + how we use them defined in onboarding

Rules for More Intentional Email Use

The key to creating more intentional communications is to create accountability within your system. I recommend that every email (or text, or chat comment, if you prefer) has one of two components: an actionable request and a yes/no-and-why response.

The **actionable request** could be a question that you need answered or an action that you're asking someone to take. When sending the message, the request should be made clearly at the outset, and *only* sent to the person or people who need to respond. Careful consideration of who you reach out to will help eliminate a lot of endless email chains and replies.

The **yes/no-and-why response** is a required answer to any email with an actionable request. You can respond "yes" with an answer to the question, a promise to find out, or an agreement to perform whatever action was requested. You can also respond with "no," but this must be accompanied with an explanation of why you cannot honor the request.

Finally, the email chain ends with a follow-up response. For a "yes," the follow-up confirms the action has been completed. For a "no-and-why," you may need to continue the dialogue to resolve the issue. But this is best done in a meeting if the discussion is more complex than an additional series of yes/no-and-why requests.

> By limiting your messaging to specific recipients
> and adding a layer of accountability, you can keep
> email from becoming a monster that feeds on every
> spare moment and saps away energy better spent on
> reaching your goals.

VIDEO CONFERENCING

Video conferencing is a critical part of the hybrid work organization. As the pandemic has clearly shown, hybrid work groups are a key component of a flexible, adaptive working environment, and they are never going to disappear.

It's important to choose a video conferencing platform that helps you create a meeting dynamic you feel comfortable with and that allows for the fluid sharing of content. Consider how you prefer to run meetings and what your expectations are for the participants. Will you need to form breakout groups? Add a chat or survey feature? Give all participants robust screen sharing? The needs of your community meetings should determine the video conferencing features you choose, and not the other way around. Again, we'll discuss more specifics of meeting design in Session 6, but for now, just be aware that your video conference system is a key part of your overall communication design.

DATA MANAGEMENT

Today's businesses rely heavily on data to make decisions about everything from supply chain management to marketing strategies. The right data technology will allow you to capture information at all points of the business. It will also allow you to store and analyze data from a central location and make it easily shareable across your organization. Your community needs to be able to access and share data to create insights and make decisions.

The right data technology will differ greatly depending on your needs, but the leader's key responsibility is to capture data, organize it, and share insights. As you choose your systems, be sure to get input from all partners and role players about how well they are able to access and share data. Leaving anyone out will mean that they cannot fully participate in your community and your mission.

COLLABORATION SOFTWARE

Not every community needs project management software, but as organizations grow and become more complex, collaboration software can become a valuable tool. The trick is to operate manually at first to develop human-to-human systems of collaboration that reflect your community's values. Your community is unique, and your members are better equipped than an external SaaS company to develop a workflow for your group.

If and when you reach the point where software will be a genuine help instead of a distraction, shop carefully for a program that fits your needs—or better yet, seek out a customizable solution. Do not try to overlay a technological system onto your human one and assume that everyone will instantly adapt. This is a recipe for a very expensive disaster, especially if your community members don't have any input into the process or the software itself.

Rewriting the Story

Think back to the story I related at the beginning of this session regarding the struggles of our friends in Chicago. They were well behind the curve on communication technology, largely because their leader was personally reluctant to learn and allowed this attitude to pervade the entire community. But in seeking to understand their technological needs, I discovered that the real problem was much bigger. Their community as a whole had not been intentionally designed to keep up with the times, and they neglected to develop a communication system that brought everyone to the table. This left out a key player—the woman who was responsible for online retail.

When I stepped in as a consultant for this organization, I knew we had to get this group to be much more intentional about the way it communicated. The first step was to invite the female e-commerce director to weekly team meetings so that the closed-off group of decision-makers could learn more about her department and its work. I also helped the leader design meeting agendas to make sure everyone was included and heard, instead of relying on loose conversation that, in the old homogenous group, just led to socializing and keeping to the status quo. The e-commerce director brought a fresh perspective and provided a good deal of information and insight that the leadership team had been lacking.

I also worked directly with the CEO to coach him on social media and how to use his iPhone more effectively. This sounds very elementary, but leadership is key, and the whole community was taking its cues about technology from this man. As he became more comfortable with the tech, he was more open to embracing a new software platform and email communication system to modernize and streamline the way the community worked together.

We had just finished implementing the bulk of these changes when the pandemic hit and all of their stores closed. Overnight, the entire business turned into an e-commerce merchant. Because they had a more open system of communication in place, the decision-makers were able to respond to the changes required. During the pandemic, their business actually *grew* because they took what they had begun and took it national. At the precise moment when everyone else was scrambling, their open communication and more intentional community building allowed them to adapt to change and achieve great success.

Next Steps

If you've done the work in this session, you are well on your way to designing your community with greater intention. Feel free to return to this session regularly as your organization grows and your needs change so that you can reassess what type of people you need to add to help you accomplish your goals. You may also want to share the candidate-centric hiring approach exercises with your partners so that it is readily available as you look for additional role players to round out your community.

Your work on the essential skill of intentionality should also have you thinking more deeply about what it means to design a community based on your values. Values are the touchstone for building your community, and we will discuss them in more detail in Session 7. In the meantime, you are free to design a communication system that brings all of your community members together and fosters open collaboration.

If you're struggling to design a system of communication, you may benefit from outside coaching or consulting. It's beyond the scope of this book to wade through every technological platform and possibility, but I've included several excellent resources and recommendations in the Appendix to steer you in the right direction.

Building a community based on shared values rather than "fit" helps you build trust. It also sends you down a new track as a leader. Instead of building an echo chamber of people who already "fit" because they look and think just like you, shared values open the door to build a truly diverse community. Embracing diversity—not the old-fashioned idea of "alignment"—is the key to the future. Once you've begun intentionally choosing your community and designing how you communicate, you're ready to build your inclusivity skills in Session 3.

INCLUSIVITY AS A SUPERPOWER

Open Your Mind and Learn to Listen

D iversity in nature, organizations, and communities creates a stronger, more sustainable system. Researchers from Darwin to cutting-edge social scientists have observed this to be the case in a wide range of animal and human communities. Because diversity is the key to healthy systems that can more readily weather challenges and change, it should be a major goal for any leader seeking to build something great. Powerful social movements around racial and gender equality, as well as remote and hybrid workforces, continue to widen the spectrum of community members in the increasingly competitive market for great talent. An inclusive culture can attract people and, more importantly, make them want to stay.

These big social changes—many of which were underway well before the pandemic, but which have definitely picked up momentum at this inflection point in history—are creating significant opportunities to increase the diversity of your community. But you can only achieve diversity if you develop the **inclusivity skills** required to attract, develop, and leverage the full potential of your workforce. A diverse workforce is not necessarily an inclusive one.

Inclusivity takes thoughtful, intentional work.

Unfortunately, most organizations have not done this work, and it shows. In the old way of doing things, people hired for "fit," which meant that they actively sought to add new community members based on their proximity to the local office and their like-mindedness. Personal networking and referrals were the keys to advancement, and this resulted in a narrow field for recruiters to select from. These networks were often quite exclusive, limited by age, gender, race, and even what college you went to.

To get a sense of what this looks like after simmering for many years, consider the US Supreme Court. Of the nine current justices, all but one earned their law degrees at Harvard or Yale, and only two were born west of the Mississippi River.[2] Though the racial and gender makeup has improved in recent years, the culture of the legal community at the highest level is still dominated by a relatively small group of people from a handful of schools.

In the business world, this lack of diversity was maintained by search firms that recruited candidates based on fit. They worked to discover what type of candidate had been successful in an organization in the past, and tailored their recruitment work to find more candidates just like that. While this priority may never have *intentionally* meant to exclude people, the results did just that. In particular, women and ethnic minorities had a difficult time being "seen" by headhunters because they didn't necessarily fit the existing mold.

And, of course, in the years before the internet and video conferencing allowed remote work, communities were further restricted by their geographic area, making it difficult for anyone who needed nontraditional hours to find their way into an established corporate culture. We now have the tools to include members of the community from around the world, yet our hiring and working practices have not caught up with this reality to create a fully inclusive environment.

---

2 "Current Members," Supreme Court of the United States, September 30, 2021, https://www.supremecourt.gov/about/biographies.aspx.

A Story: Doing What Is Right

I will be the first to admit that my own background in inclusivity work is not as robust as I wish it were. Looking back at my work as a CEO, there's a lot that I did well to ensure that my community felt empowered to share unique ideas and diverging opinions. But from the vantage point of today, I realize that I could have done more—and that I want to do more in the future. I also want to acknowledge the fact that, as an older white male, I should absolutely turn my attention to listening rather than pontificating when it comes to diversity and inclusion.

That's why I turned to Justin Jones-Fosu for help with this chapter. Justin is an inspiring speaker, writer, and consultant with incredible skills in the area of inclusivity. Justin is the author of *The Inclusive Mindset*, a deeply reflective work that guides leaders to embrace and incorporate inclusivity into their everyday lives as well as in the workplace.

Justin shared with me a great story about one of his recent corporate projects. Justin was hired by the Diversity Committee of a large US construction and engineering company. This committee was made up of a group of employees from all levels of the organization, from frontline workers to upper-level managers. Coincidentally, a new CEO was starting work there just as Justin began his consulting partnership.

An inclusivity project usually begins with a kickoff day where the CEO makes a speech.

about the importance of diversity. After those rousing words, the typical CEO hands the microphone to the consultant and in short order leaves the room—and the process. The CEO gets back to Very Important Work, while the consultant and the rest of the community are assigned to complete their diversity and inclusion tasks.

Justin calls this "lip service," and it isn't good enough.

But that didn't happen this time. The new CEO stayed in the room throughout the whole morning session and participated with the other employees in all of the exercises. He stayed through lunch and the full afternoon session as well.

His presence did not go unnoticed. Everyone involved saw that this new leader showed up and threw himself into the process. By rolling up his sleeves and diving in, elbow-to-elbow with the rest of his community, he made it clear that inclusivity was an important value to uphold.

According to Justin, leadership presence and follow-up is critical to his inclusivity work. This is especially true when a leader is attempting to create sustainable change in an organization. The goal is to make this initiative more than the work of a single day. It needs to continue into the next week and then the next month and year, until eventually inclusivity has become a core value of the organization.

Justin's initiative at the construction and engineering company was ultimately successful because the entire community focused on making a change in their culture and committed themselves to the effort—and they did it *together*. They created a new core value for the organization, which they call simply "Doing what is right."

This was an amazing way for a new CEO to become part of an organization and not just remain its figurehead. The company continues to thrive and focus on inclusivity with various follow-up programs to keep this value at the center of their work and their spirit.

Diversity and Inclusion Are Different

The words *diversity* and *inclusion* are so often paired together that they've become practically synonymous in common usage. But they are actually two different things, so it's worthwhile to explore what each means.

Diversity is a state of being that describes the makeup of your community. Diversity is a spectrum, so you can have a group like the Old Boys Club I talked about in Session 2, which has low diversity, or you can have a community with high diversity, with members from different genders, races, geographic locations, etc.

Inclusivity, on the other hand, is not a state of being so much as a mindset—and the actions that develop from that mindset. An inclusive community is one that's open to new ideas and new people, and the challenges that these differences can sometimes bring. An inclusive mindset is what will allow you to create a more diverse community because people of all backgrounds will feel welcome, heard, and valued.

Inclusivity often leads to diversity, but diversity alone does not lead to inclusivity. That requires conscious, ongoing effort that begins at the top, as our story above illustrated.

In the story of the Old Boys Club, we saw an example of how a failure to include younger, female staff led to serious dysfunction for one company. But that's not the only type of workplace diversity that needs to be addressed by today's leaders. Your work community will eventually reflect all kinds of differences present in our increasingly diverse society, including the following:

- Race

- Ethnicity

- Gender

- Sexual orientation

- Socioeconomic status

- Age

- Religious beliefs (or lack thereof)

- Geographic location (i.e., the growing hybrid and remote workforce)

Remember, you may already have a diverse community, but the mere existence of diversity does not mean that everyone feels heard, valued, and welcome. The skill of inclusivity is required to harness the strengths and leverage all of the opportunities that exist in your community.

This is crucial in today's increasingly competitive market for great talent. The pandemic led many workers to reassess their priorities, and they now wield more power over employers than we've seen in decades. A truly inclusive work culture will help you attract and retain talent, and you'll open your doors to a wider range of team members and role players to help your community grow and thrive.

Developing the skill of inclusivity begins with honest self-assessment. If you completed the self-assessment work in Session 1, you probably already have a good idea of your relative strengths and weaknesses in this area. If you have not completed this work, I encourage you to go back and do so now.

The key question to consider as you reflect is this:

Do you have an inclusive mindset?

Creativing inclusivity can feel challenging and even a bit scary because it requires constant support from you as a leader. You will need to monitor your own thoughts and actions to serve as an example of an inclusive mindset for your team. You will also need to develop an intentional strategy to enact inclusivity as part of your organization's culture. Your work in Sessions 1 and 2 have naturally built momentum to propel you into the work of inclusivity—the foundational leadership skill that you must master to steer your organization out of the past and into the future.

To develop an inclusive mindset for you, your partners, and your role players, I've developed a workflow to direct your energies toward positive results. Think of this workflow as a sluice that redirects a river. There's plenty of power in the water, but much of it is lost as it tumbles over rocks and splashes against the shore. When you build the right systems to channel your team's energy, you empower *all* players to propel your organization in exciting new directions.

Inclusivity Workflow

Step One: Develop an Inclusive Mindset

As the leader of your community, you will need to develop an inclusive mindset for yourself, of course. But inclusivity must also be embraced and practiced by *everyone*, including your partners, key decision-makers, and role players throughout your organization—right down to agencies, freelancers, and anyone you hire to help you along the way. Your chain is only as strong as its weakest link, so it's critical that everyone is part of the process of building and maintaining a culture of inclusivity.

This is important work, and it takes time. I also find it helpful to approach this work in four distinct ways to break down this big task into more manageable pieces.

TASK ONE: LISTEN, THINK, QUESTION

When you are working with someone you are actively seeking to include in your community, your work always begins with listening. Listen to what this person is saying: about their idea, their experience, their needs. Before you can act, you must understand. And the *first step to understanding is listening.*

Listening provides two big benefits. First, it shows that you value the person who is speaking because you are providing your undivided attention. Second, it's how you're going to learn what you need to know to make good decisions.

Once you have listened, *take the time to think.* Too often we pretend to be listening, when really we're just preparing our next statement in our minds. But real listening requires that you take the time to process what you've heard—especially when it has challenged your long-held beliefs or provides you with information that you had not previously considered. It's easy to feel pressure as a leader to respond immediately and act quickly, but this often backfires when it comes to inclusion. No one likes being told how they feel or what their experience has been like. A moment of thoughtful silence or even asking for a break to process what you've heard is far more effective than responding right away.

Once you've processed, *ask questions.* Taking the time to think allows you to carefully formulate your questions to be thoughtful, productive, and kind. Skillful questions are another way to honor the speaker and show them they've been heard. They will also get you deeper into the information you need to move forward.

And, of course, once you ask the question, you begin the process anew. **Listen, think, question** is an action loop that great leaders practice regularly, no matter what the topic of discussion. It's a game changer when it comes to shifting to a culture of inclusivity.

TASK TWO: CREATE A SHAME-FREE ENVIRONMENT

As you embark on the work of inclusion in your community, be careful to avoid shaming anyone. Diversity and inclusion workshops get a bad reputation for "blaming and shaming" some community members based on their position in the majority group and/or singling out others as examples of minority groups. For example, consider our Old Boys Club. We were careful never to call them sexist or try to shame them for their blind spots. That would have immediately closed every mind at the table, and we would have gotten nowhere. Instead, we kept the conversations open and focused on incremental actions that would take them from where they were to where they needed to be.

Likewise, it would have been equally unproductive to single out the lone female employee as an example who had the burden of standing for all women. Even if that type of conversation is initially well intended, it actually would have served to further isolate her by making her feel "other" than everyone else. The work of inclusivity is not about shame, but about meeting people where they are and building from there to reach a better, more open future.

TASK THREE: PROMOTE RELATIONSHIPS

As a leader, you have the power to promote relationships between people who are very different from one another. It's easy to allow different departments to become siloed away from each other in the interest of streamlining their work, but you're missing a golden opportunity for inclusion if you allow certain people to always work together while only seeing others at a quarterly meeting.

Consider ways in which you can create new working partnerships or small groups to develop new projects. It's often quite useful to get input from across departments as you work on a new initiative, but you can take this a step further by being more intentional about who you assign to work together. Does a group span ages, races, genders, and experience levels? Are your freelancers brought in early on projects? How can you bring people together who have never collaborated before?

People tend to stay where they are most comfortable, but intentionally promoting different working relationships gives everyone a chance to connect and grow. It's also the best way to ensure that you are always hearing a wide range of ideas and insights to innovate and solve problems.

TASK FOUR: DEVELOP TARGETS

Finally, as you work your way through the tasks in this workflow and the next, you'll be better positioned to open your community to invite new members of different backgrounds. As you prepare to do that, consider who you're trying to include. Does your current group lack younger workers? Do you have trouble attracting candidates of color? Do you need to round out your ranks with contract workers in the busy season?

Knowing who you need or want to include will help you define your goals and drive future actions, both in hiring and in your ongoing work to build an ever-more inclusive culture.

Step Two: Work On Your Words

Once you've worked on your own inclusivity mindset and have brought the idea to the table for the rest of your community, it's time to bring that internal work out into the world. The way we begin to put our new thinking into practice begins with the words we use. The language your community uses is one of the most important ways you demonstrate your culture. <u>How you speak—both on record in your branding materials and internally in your day-to-day work—shows your values to the world and to each other.</u>

The language of your community should, above all, bring people together. This begins with strong modeling from leaders who are careful to use words that include rather than exclude, as well as words that exemplify the values of your culture.

But what words should you use? Our language is rife with phrases from the past that developed in a time when many people were excluded from power. For example, consider the term "master bedroom." This term is so common that we don't often pause to think of where it came from. *Who*, exactly, is the master of this house, and who serves him? Do we want to live in a house with that type of power structure? Or is there another term we can use to move past those old, painful hierarchies?

More importantly, how does your community feel about the words you use every day? Language is, itself, a collaborative human endeavor, and changing it by fiat doesn't work. You'll need to work together with your community to develop norms around language that help everyone feel included. You can begin this work with the language workshop that follows.

COMMUNITY LANGUAGE WORKSHOP

1. Think about yourself and the many communities you belong to.
   How do you prefer to describe yourself?
   Use the chart below to help you get started.

   Sex/Gender/Pronouns

   Age/Generation

   Race

   Ethnicity

   Job Title

   Anything else?

2. Now think about how others describe you and the many identities you
   encompass. What are some words others might use to describe you?
   Add them to the chart below.

   Sex/Gender/Pronouns

   Age/Generation

   Race

   Ethnicity

   Job Title

   Anything else?

3. Finally, which, if any, of the expressions above are hurtful to you?
   Do any make you feel excluded? Put a line through these.

Once your fellow community members have completed this work for
themselves, you can work together to share your ideas and decide what
words make the most sense for your community to embrace—and which
ones you collectively agree to retire from your shared language.

A Word About Pronouns

Just as the way we work is rapidly evolving, so too is the language we use. One of the biggest changes is the use of pronouns to more accurately reflect a person's gender identity. The traditional way of thinking about the gender binary left room only for male and female, and speakers used he/him or she/her pronouns based on their own assumptions about a person's gender.

Today, the idea of the gender binary has been expanded from a stark either/or proposition to more of a continuum that allows people to more freely express themselves. The greater visibility of transgender men and women as well as people who identify as non-binary means that our thinking about pronouns is changing. With a wide array of gender expressions in the world, it's no longer up to the speaker to decide how to identify someone. It's up to the individual to choose the words that best describe their identity.

As with all matters of inclusivity, the key is to *listen*. When someone identifies the pronouns they'd like you to use, the right thing to do is to use those preferred words. If you forget or accidentally use the wrong pronoun, apologize and correct yourself in the moment. You might also consider normalizing pronoun use by adding preferred pronouns to work email signatures and creating norms around pronoun use when you work on your words.

For more information about gender inclusivity in the workplace, see the Appendix.

Step Three: Encourage Participation

The work of inclusion should, by definition, include as many diverse voices and perspectives as possible. It's the only way to make sure that the choices you make are ones that will actually make people feel valued. Again, we want to avoid telling people what they need, want, or deserve, and instead start listening when they tell us about themselves.

To focus your work, you'll want to ask your community for participation. While eventually everyone will participate in meetings, discussions, and workshops, it's helpful to begin with a committee or work group to get focused. This group (which, again, should be as diverse as possible!) should develop specific goals for the work as well as metrics for success and a time frame for completion.

As a leader, it's not entirely up to you to name inclusion goals. Instead, this is a golden opportunity to turn the discussion over to your community and to listen to what they need. The three big questions to answer when embarking on this work are:

- What do we want when it comes to diversity and inclusion?

- What would success in that area look like?

- How long will it take to get there?

Addressing these areas will allow your committee to approach the work of inclusion as a real project, with clear goals and metrics to guide your community as you decide how best to proceed.

Step Four: Be the Example

Though the whole community must come together to create a culture of inclusion, your role as a leader is still crucial. You must serve as an example of the inclusive culture you wish to create.

Your example is crucial to set the tone and expectations for the success of your inclusion goals. The reason so many diversity and inclusion projects fail is because businesses hire an outside consultant to do a training and disappear. Everyone takes their medicine, and then everyone goes back to what they've always done. But when the leader takes responsibility and ownership to keep the changes in place, cultures can and do improve.

This is not to say that you must be perfect at this. We all make mistakes, especially when trying something that can feel so radically new. But you should strive to be consistent with your community's goals at all times. Do your best, apologize when you fall short, keep listening, and keep trying.

Next Steps

In many ways, your work to build an inclusive leadership mindset is a continuation of the important self-reflection you began in Session 1. This work takes the mindset you have developed internally and begins to move it outward to your community. As you all come together around what it means to be open to others and their unique experiences and insights, you are building a culture. Intentionally fostering inclusivity is the key to making sure that culture is both vibrant and sustainable.

As you begin this work, you'll have to assess the state of your community. Are they willing to do this work? Are they ready? Are you? This step is too important to skip over, because culture is everything. But you may discover that you need additional help to get started or to work through thorny issues that are holding your people back when it comes to connecting fully with each other.

If you need help with the work of inclusion, there are many excellent coaches and materials available. Please see the Appendix for additional resources to guide you through this ongoing work.

The work of inclusion is never done—you will renew your commitment every day in the words you choose and in the ways you behave within your community. But if you've completed this workflow and have begun to think deeply about making changes, you're ready to share your vision with your group and with the world. The work of communication begins in Session 4.

SHARING YOUR VISION

Develop and Communicate Your Priorities

U p to this point, our work has been twofold: developing self-awareness and becoming more inclusive of others to create and lead a diverse team. The next step is to bring these two worlds—the inner world of the self and the outer world of your community—together to create an integrated whole. This is made possible by what is perhaps the most important, yet most overlooked, leadership skill: communication.

It seems so obvious on the surface that leaders need to be strong communicators to be effective, so why do so many struggle with this basic skill?

It all stems from the way leaders were developed in the past. In most large organizations, leaders were high performers who were promoted from within. For example, perhaps a great software engineer would be made the lead engineer for a whole company. The logic of this system relies on the assumption that the best performer would just naturally level up the performance of an entire department or organization.

But the mechanism by which that would occur was never fully developed. Would that leader simply improve things by being an outstanding example of success? Are they the hardest working, and therefore would be able to muscle through any problem by sheer intellectual force? In practice, this leader's education and natural inclinations had, perhaps for decades, all been focused on the single task of software engineering, and no additional leadership training would be provided.

This set up a very high-stakes, sink-or-swim system in which new leaders were thrown into the work with no support. And without understanding how to develop and communicate their vision to their teams, they would often struggle, leading to many of the common issues we see today in corporate culture: inefficiency, low morale, interpersonal conflict, and an inability to change course in the face of change.

Of course, it's not just engineers who struggle with the demands of leadership. Entrepreneurs with a great idea, floor nurses who become hospital managers, and brilliant sales-people will all struggle to lead if they haven't been trained to communicate with their communities.

This old model of leadership development is unsustainable, both for the organization and the individual tapped to step up. Businesses will suffer from lower productivity as leaders try to get up to speed, and leaders themselves will burn out because they lack the skills they need to work with increas-ingly diverse teams. In the past, leaders without strong com-munication skills could succeed simply because their teams were so homogenous that their ideas were rarely challenged. Hiring for "fit" meant that leaders were working with groups that were so much like them that they didn't have to work too hard to make their ideas understood.

But in today's world, diversity, not homogeneity, is the strength to develop. Leaders who want to develop a culture of inclusivity need highly developed communication skills that allow them to bring together diverse members to work together toward a common, well-understood vision.

our goals need strong communication [handwritten margin note]

A Story: The Merchant

Back in 2019, I was brought in to consult with a women's sportswear company. This was a large business with stores all over the country, and the new CEO wanted help develop-ing a digital marketing project to further expand their reach.

Sandy had achieved great success in the company and rose up the ladder quickly. Her original role was as a merchant and product specialist. In the world of retail fashion, merchants are key to a brand's success. Remember, these are the people who read the tea leaves of trends and decide what to buy to fill their stores. Their work is high risk and high reward, as they need to accurately predict what people will want to wear a year in advance and make investments accordingly.

Sandy excelled at this, and she loved the work. She had a strong competitive spirit and enjoyed the adrenaline rush of picking a winner. And because she was so good at this work, she eventually became the CEO. After all, if she had such an incredible eye for fashion and the business sense to know what would sell, surely she would take the entire company to the next level, right?

As I did my preliminary review of the company and each of its departments, it quickly became clear that, aside from the buying department, very few people in the organization actually interacted with Sandy regularly. Most people didn't know her well at all. This was surprising because, though Sandy was new in the position of CEO, she had been with the company for years and always spoke passionately about their product.

As I got to know Sandy better, I could see that she was struggling. She loved buying and selling and had a vast technical understanding of the company's performance numbers. But for much of Sandy's career, this was solo work. She had never been asked to communicate across departments, and she was not comfortable or fluent with other areas of the business: marketing, finance, logistics, and the day-to-day operations in the retail stores.

Because Sandy didn't have strong communication skills, she tended to avoid initiating important conversations with different departments. Sandy was largely a hands-off leader who let each department do its own thing. She did invite everyone to a biweekly update meeting in which each department would briefly share what they were working on, but that was it. Sandy's community members were never sure how their updates fit into the larger picture, and there was no mechanism for ongoing communication among departments or shared projects for them to pursue.

And then, overnight, the pandemic forced Sandy to shut down every retail store and furlough the majority of her workforce. Sandy suddenly found herself the leader of a small remote team, making decisions based on a constantly changing scenario. To do that effectively, Sandy needed a high level of shared awareness with her team. She needed to work closely with operations and marketing to understand what was necessary, what was possible, and how long changes would take to implement.

How would Sandy, who already struggled with communication skills and had no strong system of communication in place, cope with the demands of the pandemic?

Three New Communication Skills to Master

It's important to note that the pandemic didn't *cause* a breakdown in communication; rather, the pandemic *revealed* weaknesses that had been simmering for decades. Up until March

2020, many leaders had been able to get by on hard work or sheer momentum. But when people were forced to work from home, it became immediately clear where the gaps in communication were. Remote work saved the day, and it provided a glimpse of the future of work. We are never going back to the way things were before, and the leaders who will thrive in this new world are the ones who develop a clear vision and the communication skills to share it with *everyone*.

So what does purposeful, effective communication of your vision look like in today's world? It's a multifaceted process that requires a great leader to develop three main skills to accomplish.

Skill One: Positivity

Positivity is the ability to transmit good feelings to others in a way that resonates with them. Whether you're brainstorming ideas, meeting challenges, executing projects, or weathering change, your positive attitude as a leader can have a major impact on your community. People take their emotional cues from their leaders, so your community is always looking to you for guidance on how to behave and interpret events.

When you radiate positivity as a leader, the rest of your community will respond in kind, which boosts morale and creates a successful working environment. This isn't just a New Age hunch either. In his book *Primal Leadership: Realizing the Power of Emotional Intelligence*, Daniel Goleman digs into the research to explain how positivity leads to productivity. He explains that when the top management team displays an overall positive mood, they experience greater cooperation, which in turn leads to better business results. When leadership displays more negativity, market performance drops accordingly.[3]

Positivity is especially important in a hybrid or remote working environment because you cannot rely on a comfortable office space or water cooler small talk to convey and maintain good feelings. In a remote environment, you must actively display positivity in your facial expressions, body language, and spoken words. Your personal attitude becomes even more significant when it's the only thing your remote working community interacts with.

Positive Affirmations

Before you meet in person or online with members of your community, it's always a good idea to check in on your emotional state. If you sense any negativity in your mood, I suggest taking a moment to take a deep breath and repeat a three-word affirmation to yourself to get into a better place.

Creating an affirmation is simple. Just choose three words that reflect the way you want to feel and present yourself to others. For example, I often use an affirmation of "calm, focused, clear" before I present to a group. You might choose something like "positive, supportive, open-minded"—or whatever you need to focus your mood into one that will have the right impact on your community.

---

3 Daniel Goleman, *Primal Leadership: Realizing the Power of Emotional Intelligence* (Boston: Harvard Business Review Press, 2013).

Skill Two: Sustainability

As we discussed in Session 1, it is crucial for leaders to develop a sustainable mindset. Sustainability refers to the energy and personal resources required to get your message across—and to keep delivering the message of your vision repeatedly and consistently over time. Now that you've embraced personal sustainability, it's time to expand that vision for your partners and community at large.

But before you can communicate your vision, you need to zero in on exactly what your message is. Creating a sustainable vision requires realistic goals and timelines that leave room for exploration, experimentation, and daily improvement. No vision can be sustainable if it requires superhuman stamina and eighty-hour workweeks to fulfill. Your vision must be clear enough for people to believe in but flexible enough to allow you to adapt to a fast-changing environment.

If you have worked on your personal sustainable mindset in Session 1, you are ready to bring those ideas to your community at large as you craft your shared vision. This core leadership skill will help you create a vision that is sustainable for your entire community, which in turn will help them all do their best work to bring it to fruition.

Skill Three: Inclusivity

In Session 3, we explored the importance of creating an inclusive environment for your community. As you develop and communicate your vision, you'll expand this inclusive attitude beyond your immediate working group to the wider community and the world at large.

An inclusive vision must benefit others, not just yourself as a leader or your shareholders. And a truly inclusive vision will benefit everyone in your community. Everyone who is working toward your goal should also benefit from their labor. An inclusive vision goes beyond dominating the market and making piles of money to providing some social benefit as well.

An inclusive vision is hugely important when it comes to attracting a diverse employee base. When potential hirees can see the broader benefits that you provide to society, they will feel included in your vision and empowered to contribute. What many leaders today fail to grasp is that in today's world, you can't simply run a company. You must build a community.

To do this, you'll need to bring positivity, sustainability, and inclusivity together into one cohesive vision.

Vision Workflow

Developing your vision is definitely a collaborative effort. It's critical to begin with an open mindset, and you'll want to work with a trusted partner, mentor, or coach to serve as a sounding board for your ideas. To use this workflow effectively, read over all the steps first. Try your hand at the exercises alone, but be sure to share your work with a partner to gather feedback and get help in your areas of weakness before sharing your vision with your community.

Step One: Clarify Your Vision

The best way I know to gain clarity and focus in your thinking is to apply the Question Progression. As we saw in Session 1, the Question Progression uses the most basic question words to drill down into the essentials of your idea. Each one is important, and though the questions are short, your answers should be thorough.

Use the Question Progression below to clarify your vision. Work on your own first, then share your answers with a partner you trust to point out any areas that lack detail or seem unrealistic.

Note that the Question Progression below can be used to clarify your thinking on any number of goals, initiatives, and problems to be solved. It's incredibly useful for big-picture vision development, but you can also put it into practice on a daily basis to help you focus on smaller issues and tasks. You might consider working through it anytime you have an important message to convey, as it will sharpen your thinking and help you create a cohesive explanation to share with your community.

THE QUESTION PROGRESSION: DEVELOPING YOUR VISION

1. **What?** What do you want to accomplish?

2. **Who?** Who will *benefit* from this work? Who will *perform* this work?

3. **Why?** Why are you doing this work? Why is it worthwhile?

4. **How?** How will this work be done? How will the process and outcomes reflect your values?

5. **When?** When do you want to achieve your goal? When will you build in time to experiment and adjust to create a sustainable timeline?

ρ Two: Prepare Your Agenda

ι my work as a consultant, I typically sit in on ten to fifteen weekly meetings as I learn about a company's internal operations and culture. Sometimes I'll call a leader an hour before the meeting to check in with them, and I've lost count of how many times they answer, "I don't know" or "My assistant has the agenda."

This just isn't good enough. As a leader, you must take a hands-on approach to preparing your own agenda and working through your talking points. Spend some time thinking about your priorities and what you want to discuss with your community on your own, and then discuss it with your partners as you create your agenda.

Once your ideas are aligned, make a good outline of what you want to discuss. This is just as important for your annual presentation as it is for weekly team meetings. Being prepared lets your audience know that you value their time, and that what you have to say is important. It will also allow you to speak more fluently in the moment.

It should be noted that making an outline is not the same as writing a speech. Reading directly from a paper actually erodes your audience's trust in you because it leaves them wondering if you are speaking your own words. It's much better to develop a few bullet points to remind you of the shape of your message but to rely on your memory for the meat of the topics encompassed by each bullet. If public speaking in this way is difficult for you, practice aloud ahead of time.

This extra preparation goes a long way to building trust with your audience.

As you speak, remember the skill of positivity. You want to radiate good energy to your community, so avoid rants. At times you may need to express anger or dissatisfaction, but it is much better to build this into a story than to rant or lecture. (More on the art of storytelling in a moment.)

Finally, build a request for feedback into your agenda. Ideally, you should begin your presentation by letting your audience know that when you're finished, you'd love to hear their point of view about what you've said. This immediately engages your audience and builds upon your culture of inclusivity—and it's a valuable tool to improve your future communications too.

Step Three: Tell Your Story

Good communication is very often supported by good storytelling. Fortunately, you don't have to be a natural poet or award-winning actor to become a skilled storyteller. All you need to do is become familiar with the elements of a great story so you can apply them to the message you wish to convey.

To my mind, a great story flows like a wave that moves fluidly between the past and the future in a way that provides context and builds momentum for your vision. I call this format the **Story Wave**:

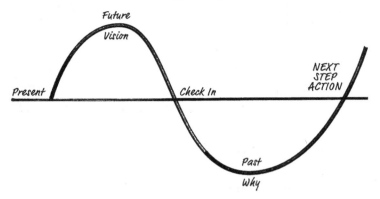

STORYLINE WAVE

Future
Vision

Present

Check In

NEXT
STEP
ACTION

Past
Why

To be meaningful to your audience, a good story begins in the present. Describing the current moment engages and includes your listeners in what you have to say. Open your story with where you are right now, including both the positive and negative aspects of this moment.

Next, take your listeners into the future. This is where you can identify potential solutions to problems, imagine new inventions, and describe the positive results that will follow from the work. In discussing the future, you are communicating your vision for what is possible.

To bring your story back into the present, pause for a check-in. Is your audience understanding your vision? Do they share your feelings? Ask for feedback midway through. This keeps your audience engaged and disarms any skeptical listeners by allowing them to say their piece earlier in the process, instead of allowing them to sit and stew with any objections. You're keeping all of your listeners involved in the story.

Next, pivot to the past. This is where you can explain the motivation behind what you're doing. What in the past inspired you to move forward to the future in the specific way you propose? Here you are sharing your purpose, so this is a great place to add a memorable personal detail to the story. This will help people remember and connect with you when it's time to move forward with your new ideas.

Finally, the story ends back in the present with the actions you will take to move into the future. As you can see in the Story Wave, the momentum of your story moves into the future at the end, which will propel your community in the direction you want them to go.

One of the most important things the Story Wave does is reframe your vision so that it's easier for your audience to grasp. Remember, you've already been mulling over a problem and coming up with an action plan for some time, so you've had the benefit of weighing all the options and developing your vision with all the available data. But your audience is hearing this for the first time, and they are naturally going to wonder how your vision came to be.

In the past, most leaders tended toward a basic problem/solution method of presenting their ideas: here's what's wrong, here's how I want you to fix it. But this has the effect of sounding like an edict from above rather than a shared vision. You could have the best solution in the world, but if you don't get buy-in from your community, your vision will fail. The Story Wave begins with a shared understanding of the present and helps guide your community to a vision of the future possibilities. It makes time to check understanding and to foster engagement, and then it provides the rationale behind the thinking by dipping into the past—and, ideally, getting personal. This creates deeper connections and helps your audience understand not only what you want from them, but why you want it and how your vision will benefit everyone.

With practice, developing a positive vision and sharing it with great storytelling will become more natural. To get better at it, you can begin to put it into practice right now, with any project or initiative you're considering. Vision is not a one-time activity. It is not a mission statement that you develop in a workshop, hang on the wall, and never speak of again.

Vision is your perception of the future. Vision is dynamic and changes with the changing times and needs of your community. It encompasses your overarching mission, your medium-term endeavors, and your day-to-day projects.

Communicating your vision is an ongoing process. It's not something you accomplish and cross off your list, but something you're always working on. With every meeting and every email, you'll be communicating your vision in ways both large and small. To be effective, you must stay positive, be prepared, and tell your story in an engaging way.

Rewriting the Story:
The Merchant Learns to Communicate

Now that you've given more thought to your vision and have undertaken the work required to build specific communication skills of positivity, sustainability, and inclusivity, let's take a look at how these skills can transform a floundering team.

When we last peeked in on Sandy, she was facing an enormous challenge with the pandemic shuttering her retail business outlets and forcing her to furlough the portion of her team that worked in stores. Remember, Sandy's strength lay in the competitive marketplace of buying and selling, and she did not have strong relationships with other department leaders within her organization.

Overnight, Sandy's company became a small remote team that had to do digitally what they were used to doing in person. My consulting practice shifted our focus from their marketing strategy to guiding them through this challenging transition.

And the key to making it work was communication.

I convinced Sandy to start a weekly all-hands video conference to keep everyone in the loop on all of the changes that were happening. This was a huge shift for Sandy personally, who really had never shown much interest in the other departments in her company because she assumed they could all run themselves without her input.

I coached Sandy on the importance of sharing her vision with all of her employees—even the furloughed ones—to keep them informed. During the uncertainty of the pandemic, this was especially crucial for the furloughed employees, who were desperate for updates about the company and their jobs. Regular communication was also key to making sure separate departments were all on the same page and could work together to coordinate their responses. In the past, Sandy was able to get away with quick one-on-one check-ins, but remote work requires intentional communication to create a cohesive team.

I helped Sandy prepare for these meetings so that she was able to communicate her vision effectively. This was a big shift for Sandy as a leader. Her focus had always been on buying and selling, and she had never had the chance to develop the skills of communication and engagement with the organization. With coaching, Sandy learned to share her vision effectively. Because the pandemic was such a volatile situation, that vision was subject to change regularly, but whether she was providing an update on reopening plans or sharing her vision for the future in a difficult time, Sandy learned to convey optimism and include all players in these meetings.

Sandy also worked to portray an optimistic vision, which was not always easy given the headlines of the day and the uncertainty of when they would be able to reopen their retail stores. She made sure everyone was engaged by having other members of the management team serve as guest speakers, and she created a real sense of community by including everyone in the conferences. Her personal journey from merchant-manager to capable leader was made possible by her commitment to building her communication skills.

Sandy's team became much stronger as a result, and her business was able to thrive. While other fashion retailers were floundering, Sandy's company was able to increase sales and rehire all of their employees within three months.

Next Steps

Though it's not traditionally thought of as a key business skill, communication is central to effective leadership at this moment in the world. With an increasingly diverse workforce and rapid changes to what it even means to perform work as a team, a leader's ability to engage and communicate with their team is a make-or-break skill.

To develop your ability to communicate your vision, remember that effective communication is built on three discrete but intertwined skills:

- **Positivity:** a culture that resonates with goodwill

- **Sustainability:** clear, flexible goals

- **Inclusivity:** engaging others in a quest that benefits the wider community

You can practice these skills by completing the Vision Workflow above. Remember, communication is ongoing, so you can return to the steps in the workflow again and again to clarify your vision as it evolves.

I would also encourage you to practice storytelling regularly. In fact, I invite you to write a story using the Story Wave practice and bring it to our community for feedback. Send your story in for comment and feedback at www.notgoingback.net.

I also encourage you to use the Question Progression whenever you are planning to communicate something with your team—no matter how small. Ideally, asking yourself What, Who, Why, and How will become second nature. When it does, you'll find that your vision is much clearer from the outset, so it becomes easy to share.

It's also a good idea to get specific feedback from your partner or mentor regarding your communication skills. Getting an honest opinion about where you have difficulty will help you zero in on the work you need to do to improve.

Finally, if you still find yourself struggling to communicate after working these skills, it's time to seek additional coaching. Check the resources in the Appendix for more guidance. It's crucial to develop your vision and improve your communication, as these skills will form the basis of your ability to adapt in the face of change.

FOCUS AND ADAPT

Set Flexible Goals to Move Forward

In the past, leadership training—if one was lucky enough to get any coaching in this area at all—tended to prioritize focus at the expense of many other skills. To build a business, the thinking went, you had to choose one area in which to excel and focus all of your attention and efforts on growth in that area. This can work well for many years, particularly in the early phases of a startup.

However, over time, groups need to be able to adapt to changing circumstances, and a too-strictly focused leadership model makes change difficult. In today's complex, fast-changing world, these two seemingly contradictory skills must be brought together. I call this skill **focused adaptability**. Thinking about focused adaptability as one coherent mindset will enable you to respond to a changing environment more nimbly while maintaining your community's core values and priorities. This balanced leadership will be crucial for success in the future.

To understand the problem with focusing solely on core competencies, consider the rise and fall of the railroads. In the late nineteenth and early twentieth century, railroads dominated American industry as *the* way to get goods and people from one place to another. Railroad tycoons were in the "tracks and trains" business, and they focused all of their attention on building more lines and faster engines. Life was good—right up until the automobile came along.

Suddenly, the railroad business was shrinking. If railroad companies had been less focused and more adaptable, they would have realized that they shouldn't have been in the "tracks and trains" business, but rather in the *transportation* business. If they had developed a more flexible outlook, they would have more easily been able to shift to keep up with the times while still maintaining their core competency as a business that moved goods—rather than one shortsightedly married to the rails.

The railroads had a good run, though—a century of dominance is nothing to sneeze at. But today, technology evolves at a much faster rate than it did in the 1800s. Likewise, the speed of communication allows the whole culture to change more quickly as well. The speed at which the world changes affects every industry, from transportation to retail, as we will see in our next story.

A Story: The Brand Builder

For a short time, I worked with a very successful CEO with a long history of building shopping centers, stores, brands, and even residential communities. He had a deep curiosity about new things and always dug into a project with passion and intensity. This was the type of person who would read every book or article he could get his hands on when a subject piqued his interest, and then synthesize all of that information into a cohesive narrative. It was fascinating to listen to him explain how something worked.

This CEO's personal strengths tended toward deep focus, which he applied to his personal learning and research. It's no exaggeration to say that focus was his dominant value in his work as well: he built a business empire by focusing specifically on what he could do best to win against any competitor.

Specifically, he was focused on store experience. He built a retail chain that provided a very specific shopping experience for customers. While in his stores, customers were treated to upscale surroundings, a refined color palette, and attentive service from attractive sales associates. This was a marked difference from the matter-of-fact way his competitors operated, and customers loved it.

His focus helped him succeed by carving out a new niche in his market, but it also eventually led to the breakup of his business. As CEO, he led a very top-down culture that did not make room for diverse opinions. The core group of executives made every decision, and they didn't invite regional managers to the table to learn about the way their stores were faring in different areas of the country.

He had built a dominant brand, but his extreme focus did not allow him to hear the rumblings of change. A regional manager in San Francisco tried to point out that the company's store experience now felt alienating to people with different gender expressions and a more flexible outlook on traditional gender roles. Fashions and social mores were changing, but he was not able to adapt because his focus blinded him to the ways in which the ground was shifting beneath his feet.

Focused Adaptability

For many years, prioritizing focus over adaptability has meant prioritizing quantifiable results—often to the exclusion of all else. Businesses focused on growing their numbers, and that in turn led them to expand, getting bigger and bigger while remaining focused on a single core competency or product category. In this model, growth has come from investment in the core or expansion into close adjacencies to the core.

But organizations built around one stationary core concept can be extremely risky in this new environment. Thanks to the internet and globalization, competitors can now come from anywhere in the world. We live in a culture in which consumers' tastes and lifestyles are changing rapidly, and it doesn't take much—as we saw in the story above—for them to abandon your brand if it no longer fits their vision of the world. And, of course, global events like pandemics, climate change, and social upheaval all force change as well—often in completely unpredictable ways.

For today's leaders, focus alone will no longer get the job done. That ship has sailed. To be an effective leader in today's environment, you must embrace focused adaptability. This is an elevated and intentional approach that requires a highly adaptive community mindset and transparent communication, as well as a constant focus on your core values.

It's important to note that an adaptive mindset comes from the leader, but it must also be embraced and adopted by the entire community. Everyone needs to be conscious of and open to the changes that are happening in the world. If you've done the work to develop an inclusive community and communicate your core values, you are ready to employ those skills here to help everyone become more flexible in the face of inevitable changes.

Adaptive Mindset Workflow

Developing an adaptive mindset is important for leaders personally, but it's also important to develop in your community as a whole. Try using this workflow as a guide to your own thinking first, then consider bringing it to your partners so you can work on these skills together. You may find it useful as a way to approach a particular problem, or you may wish to use it to guide your overall approach to decision-making and communication within your community.

As your leadership team begins to develop and model an adaptive mindset, it will ideally become part of your overarching community culture. This requires commitment, but the benefits of being able to react flexibly in the face of change are priceless.

Step One: Separate Values from Opinions

Your values are who you are, not what you do. No matter what happens in the world, your values should not change. If you have already completed the Vision Workflow in Session 4, you should have a better sense of your values. If you haven't done that work, I invite you to return to the Question Progression in Session 4 to think deeply about your values. Your values define your community and will serve as a beacon to guide your ship across stormy seas.

Opinions and ideas, on the other hand, can and should change as the situation evolves. You should remain open to hearing divergent opinions and experimenting with new ideas, as these will help you change to meet the moment. Opinions about how best to carry out your values will change; the values themselves will not. This will give your entire community the confidence to explore the next steps.

Step Two: Develop Mental Flexibility

Mental flexibility will allow you to hear all the new opinions and ideas that you've worked so hard to be open to. A key requirement is curiosity. Instead of resisting change, try to learn all you can about what's coming your way. In meditation, this attitude is called "beginner's mind." It's a posture in which you try to observe everything as if you have never seen it before. What makes it tick? What can you learn from it?

Scientists and designers are experts at this. They form an idea and then test it to see what works and what doesn't. Experimentation means that sometimes something won't work, but an attitude of mental flexibility lets you use that feedback to get better instead of shying away from possible failure. This willingness to reevaluate and change your perceptions is what allows you to adapt.

Step Three: Practice Transparent Communication

To support a culture of focused adaptability, it's important to keep the lines of communication open so people understand both what is happening around them and their role in it. Transparent communication is not merely frequent, however. It's also *two way.*

This means asking for feedback from all members of your community and allowing your assumptions to be challenged. In fact, you should actively ask for new opinions. This is especially important in a remote or hybrid working environment and in a diverse community where you need to work even harder to ensure all voices are heard. Allowing yourself to be open and vulnerable to your community helps establish trust and gives everyone the confidence to speak up. Ultimately, this will drive new ideas and solutions—but first, you have to be willing to admit your imperfections and lack of knowledge.

Step Four: Keep at It

If the idea of admitting your mistakes and weaknesses to your entire community feels challenging—well, it is. You will not be perfect at transparent communication at first. Nor will it always be easy to practice mental flexibility. But you can get better at these steps over time to develop a stronger focused adaptability mindset.

Like many of the skills we've discussed in this book, focused adaptability is not a one-and-done activity. Instead, it's something you continually develop over time. So find ways to actively experiment in your work. Try new ideas, see where they lead, and learn from your mistakes. And then do it again and again. When you model this type of resilience for your community, you're letting them know that you value flexibility and experimentation—and you'll inspire them to do more of it.

Adaptive Community Design Workflow

Once you have begun the internal work of building a focused, adaptive mindset for yourself and your partners, it's time to build this skill outward to the rest of your community. By now this rhythm should feel familiar, as our work in previous sessions has begun with the self and then moved to the community at large.

Intentionally designing an adaptive community takes work, in large part because organizations have historically not valued flexibility and openness. Your community members may not naturally join you with these skills, but you can work to develop them together.

Step One: Define Your Core

Who are you as a community, and what defines you? Getting everyone on board with your core provides the firm foundation for all of your work. Once your community is clear on your core, they will feel more confident in proposing experiments and ideas that enhance it.

Answer the questions below to develop your core.

1. Why does your community exist?

2. For businesses, what products or services are most essential
    to your community? For nonprofits, what is your mission?

3. What makes your community distinctive or unique?

Your answers to the questions above should provide a solid basis
for a brief statement of your core values. This is an important
clarifying statement that should be developed as a community
and clearly presented to all by the leader.

Here's an example of a complete values statement that I've
developed with The Ember Company, my consulting firm:

We exist because the traditional consulting model no longer works for companies of today.

Our core business is helping companies envision and execute on potential growth strategies that are outside of their internal capabilities.

We are made up of former business leaders that have specific experience and insight into our partners' needs.

Our values are Transparency, Efficiency, and Proactivity.

Take a moment to consolidate your answers above into a cohesive statement that will guide the rest of your work.

4.   Our Values Statement:

Step Two: Develop a Culture of Transparent Communication

If you've done the work in Session 2 and Session 4, you should be well on your way toward designing a community that embraces transparent communication, but I mention it here again because this is critical, ongoing work. Remember that your communication should be:

- Honest

- Timely

- Frequent

- Two way

A culture of transparent communication means that the entire community is on a need-to-know basis. When you keep everyone in the loop—particularly about changes—you build the trust you need to move quickly when circumstances demand it.

Step Three: Evaluate All Change through the Lens of Your Core

As the world changes around you, your community will need to adapt. But how do you know that you are making good decisions together? Keep your core at the forefront of decision-making, and it will serve as your guide.

Whenever you face change in your community, ask yourselves this question:

How does this change affect our core?

Change can come in two forms: it can happen to you, or you can choose it. Externally forced changes include demographic shifts, a change in your customer base or competition, technological advances, global events, and social change. Consider how these events affect your core, then ask yourself how your responses—the changes you *choose* to make—will affect your core as well. This single question, answered thoughtfully, holds the key to making effective change that your community agrees upon and supports.

Step Four: Set Clear Priorities and Achievable Goals

In order to adapt successfully and make necessary changes, your community needs to share a unified vision of success. This is especially important in a remote or hybrid working environment, where many community members will not have a clear view of how their part in the work ties into the whole unless you explicitly tell them. The question that guides your goal setting is this:

What are you all working toward, and how will you know when you've achieved it?

In the past, organizational planning was based on a timetable, typically in the form of five-year plans. But because change is now happening all around us, all the time, being chained to a long-term plan doesn't provide enough flexibility to adapt. It's better to work with shorter-term goals or sprints that will allow you to solve problems and experiment with new ideas without tying up resources indefinitely.

Step Five: Support Experimentation

While your community remains focused on your priorities and goals, remember to balance that focus with adaptability. The best way to do this is by creating a culture of experimentation. When you allow your community to try out new ideas in support of your priorities, you build mutual trust and a culture of open idea sharing.

Successful experiments can then be incorporated into your daily work or turned into new priorities. This openness fosters an attitude of continuous learning and improvement that will permeate your culture, leading to the percolation of great new ideas as well as a can-do attitude when circumstances require even bigger changes. Some of the best ideas come from the people on the front lines, so be sure to ask for input—and then listen to the answers!—instead of implementing change from the top down.

THE ADAPTABLE FOCUS MATRIX

Balancing priorities and experimentation can be challenging—if it weren't, leaders everywhere would already be adept at focused adaptability. The matrix below is designed to help organize your thinking and guide your communication with your community. When everyone sees the big picture of your priorities, they will know how best to move the community forward.

To keep track of your current initiatives so you can clearly communicate what is a priority and what is a new idea worth exploring, use this adaptable focus matrix.

PRIORITIES

Priorities are major initiatives that your whole community is always striving toward. These could include basics like growing your reach and increasing revenue or important new initiatives that are required to get you where you want to go. All members of your community should be included in and clear on your priorities.

Priority 1:   Goals/Benchmarks:

                           Time Frame:

                           Quantifiable Result:

Priority 2:   Goals/Benchmarks:

                           Time Frame:

                           Quantifiable Result:

Priority 3:   Goals/Benchmarks:

                           Time Frame:

                           Quantifiable Result:

PROJECTS

Projects are important new initiatives that smaller groups within your community undertake together. These projects are designed to further develop your future priorities as listed above. As emerging projects grow and take on a life of their own, they may become the priorities of tomorrow.

Project 1:	Goals/Benchmarks:
	Time Frame:
	Quantifiable Result:
Project 2:	Goals/Benchmarks:
	Time Frame:
	Quantifiable Result:
Project 3:	Goals/Benchmarks:
	Time Frame:
	Quantifiable Result:

EXPERIMENTS

Experiments are new ideas that are often generated by younger community members and others who may be working under the radar in your community. These ideas are worth trying in a small, fast test environment, and leaders should listen to the results carefully. Note that goals aren't listed here, as they should remain highly flexible in the spirit of true experimentation.

Experiment 1:	Goals/Benchmarks:
	Time Frame:
	Quantifiable Result:
Experiment 2:	Goals/Benchmarks:
	Time Frame:
	Quantifiable Result:
Experiment 3:	Goals/Benchmarks:
	Time Frame:
	Quantifiable Result:

A Word About Communities in Transition

It's important to remember that significant change can create a fear of loss in your community. Strong emotions of anger, grief, and powerlessness are real, and they cannot be ignored. When you are forced, or perhaps choose, to make major changes in your community, truth and trust are the keys to executing transitions quickly. If you're doing the work in these sessions, you're already building the trust. During any transition, you'll also need to rely on your transparent communication skills to tell the truth to your community, even when it may be painful to do so.

Though change management is beyond the scope of this book, I've included some helpful resources in the Appendix to help you navigate difficult transitions and upheaval in your community.

Rewriting the Story

What ever happened to our story's CEO, the talented brand builder from the beginning of this session? His extreme focus was a double-edged sword. On one hand, he was a wizard at creating a retail experience that made shopping hugely appealing for his customers. On the other hand, that singular focus—and, it must be said, a fair amount of ego—meant that he was unable or unwilling to react to cultural changes. Unfortunately, his top-down leadership style made it impossible for these new ideas to break through, and his business was broken into several different companies.

But it didn't have to be that way, and I'd love to rewrite the ending of this story. If he had developed the skill of focused adaptability, he would have created a community in which diverse opinions were welcomed. This would have created an opportunity for that smart regional manager in San Francisco to speak freely about the changes they were seeing on the ground: Which customers were no longer coming in to shop? What weren't they buying, and what were they asking for instead?

With those questions out there, this CEO could then have turned to his community for ideas about how to work with these changes. Could buyers experiment with a new line aimed at the disaffected customers? Could store designers pilot a new look and run a pilot in a few major cities? What other ideas would his community have brought to the table if given the chance?

Next Steps

In this session, we have seen that the traditional business skill of focusing on the core cannot, by itself, guarantee success. The pace of change in the world is simply too fast and unpredictable for that to work any longer. To be successful today, leaders must pair their focus with a culture of adaptability. This work begins with the leader's personal mindset and expands outward to the community culture at large.

Once you have completed the workflows in this session, you should be well equipped to guide your community to focus on core priorities *and* experiment with new ideas. This is an ongoing process, so do refer to this session periodically, especially when your community faces change.

You may have noticed that several themes from earlier sessions have emerged in this session's work. If you are not yet comfortable with your inclusivity and communication skills, you can always reengage with the work in earlier sessions to support your focused adaptability.

In our next session, we will dig deeper into one of the most overlooked communication skills of all: the design and execution of a good meeting.

YES, MEETINGS

Create and Lead Functional Meetings

Let's begin by acknowledging an important truth: meetings have a reputation for being awful. They're reviled as massive time wasters, and this is unfortunately true of *bad* meetings. But good meetings are a way for leaders to share their vision, add insight to data, and get important feedback from the community at large. A right-sized meeting that begins with a purpose-driven agenda, includes idea sharing, and ends with clear decisions and actions has always been effective.

The question, then, isn't *Should I have meetings?* Of course you should! Meetings are a foundational part of any transparent, inclusive communication plan. The big question for today's leaders is:

What is the role of the well-designed meeting in my community?

In the past, meetings were often a hierarchically driven, lecture hall-like experience, where managers made announcements and collected quick updates from different departments. In the worst case scenarios, these meetings were long and largely off-the-cuff, with managers improvising the agenda as they went. Meeting attendees could sense the lack of preparation, which of course made them wonder whether the meeting was actually important or necessary. Since they had no opportunity to share ideas or provide feedback, the meetings never got any better—and morale would tick down every time the team walked into the conference room. Rinse and repeat.

Fast-forward to today, and advancements in data aggregation and team collaboration software have made communication among teams much more effective and efficient. Teams can integrate critical content, updates, resources, and calendars with just a few keystrokes and stay connected to work onsite or asynchronously as needed. They're also able to share and present data in a customized format across the entire community.

This new technology is ideal for keeping remote and hybrid teams informed and aligned, but future success will require more than just access to information. Unfortunately, collaboration platforms can also create silos and echo chambers where teams or departments work very closely together but fail to share their processes across departments, leading to mini-fiefdoms within what should be one community.

Though technology has solved some of the problems of meetings by making it easier to share information, it has also created new problems. Bringing together a diverse group of in-person and remote workers and keeping both internal and external role players up-to-date requires a new approach to meetings. Intentional meeting design is the key to bringing all of the leadership skills you've worked on in previous sessions together as you move forward with your community.

A Story: The Hub

In my consulting work, I'm often hired to work on one specific area of a business. However, the work pivots and grows as the situation requires, often after my assessment of a company reveals deeper issues than what the CEO initially presented. This isn't because these CEOs are trying to hide anything from me. It's because they have blind spots that have grown into issues that permeate the community as a whole.

One such blind spot recently came to light in my work with a specialty foods company. Though I was initially brought on to complete a straightforward digital transformation project, the work changed dramatically when the company's CEO quit just two weeks before I began. Because the community was now leaderless, I suddenly found myself dealing with all aspects of the business in an effort to right the ship while the founder searched for a new leader.

One of my most important assessment tools is to sit in on company meetings. This allows me to observe the leader's personal style and see the community's culture in action. Since the CEO was gone, none of these meetings were happening. In an effort to piece together clues about the former leader's strategies, I asked his assistant for a copy of his calendar.

What I saw was astonishing.

Every Monday through Wednesday, the CEO's calendar was booked with wall-to-wall meetings. Starting at 8:00 a.m., he met for an hour with each of his department heads individually. One of these meetings was a lunch meeting so that he could fit eight to ten meetings into his day and leave the office by six. (I'm honestly not sure when he found time for a bathroom break.) The frazzled assistant kept track of each of these interactions in a notebook for the CEO.

On the surface, this might seem like the work of an incredibly hands-on CEO, and in some ways, it was. But these were the *only* meetings occurring in this community. There were no meetings among department heads, and no all-hands meetings. Each department had its own Slack channel, but there was no system of communication by which departments could share information.

The result of this system was a colossal waste of time for the CEO, who had made himself the hub of all information flowing through his company. *He* knew what was going on, and made sure that each department was doing its job, but the result was that he had very little time for anything other than meetings and check-ins. He saw himself as the facilitator of information flow, but he had no system in place for empowering his teams to actually work with that data. The department heads had no idea what was going on in other parts of the company, so they couldn't collaborate or solve problems. They barely even knew each other's names, much less what they were working on.

It's no wonder that this CEO burnt out and left behind a company that functioned less like a community and more like an archipelago of islands in an unbridgeable sea.

Effective Meeting Workflow

If you've done all of the leadership work in the previous sessions, you are well prepared with the skills that underpin a good meeting: listening, inclusivity, communication. But crafting a good meeting—one that brings everyone together and uses their time wisely—requires some very specific additional skills.

Step One: Plan Your Meeting Calendar

First, great meetings don't just happen. They are planned. Part of any good leader's transparent communication plan should include a meeting calendar that clearly outlines the type of meeting and who is participating—in addition to providing as much advance notice to participants as possible.

The type of meeting you plan depends on what you wish to achieve. There are five basic styles of meetings, each one with a different purpose:

- **All-Hands Meetings:** This is a weekly review of key results, important data points, shared insights, and learnings from emerging issues. Everyone in the community attends and participates. Ideally, the all-hands meeting occurs at a standard date and time so everyone can plan around it. It should be a main component of your community's working rhythm.

- **Brainstorm Breakouts:** A smaller group from diverse areas focuses on a specific problem to solve or opportunity to pursue. These are often temporary groups that come together for a specific purpose and report back to the community at the next all-hands meeting. This smaller, ad hoc group is more nimble, so brainstorm breakouts are ideal for conducting background research, gaining clarity on an issue, and generating a first round of ideas around it.

- **Functional Group Alignment:** Another smaller group of people come together around a particular area of execution: marketing, logistics, finance, sales, etc. In the past, these were often viewed as "department meetings," but today's working environment requires an expanded view that focuses on the *function* rather than the job title. It's crucial to also include agencies, freelancers, and people from other areas who work closely on any particular function.

- **One-on-One Meetings:** These meetings help build deeper relationships and are particularly useful in providing feedback, coaching, and mentorship. In the past, these meetings were often left to chance encounters in the break room or scheduled only in a time of crisis, but today's leaders must intentionally incorporate them into their planning to foster good relationships in the community. In particular, one-on-one meetings help keep remote workers engaged and connected to your vision.

- **Project Huddle:** This is a tactical meeting focused on bringing together anyone working on a particular project. While a function group is focused on the big picture of their work, a project huddle is all about getting a particular job done. There are only three questions to ask and answer in a project huddle:

- What did I do last week?

- What am I working on now?

- What kind of help do I need?

As you plan your meeting calendar, begin with the all-hands, then work with your partners to develop a mutually agreeable cadence for functional group alignment meetings.

From there, determine what your needs are right now. Are you working on a specific project? Do you want to empower experimentation? How can you schedule one-on-one meetings to connect with others? The answers to these questions will drive the scheduling and planning of project huddles, brainstorming breakouts, and one-on-one meetings in the way that works best for your community.

Step Two: Create the Agenda

Once you have a meeting on your calendar, you need to plan it. Every meeting you conduct must have a clear purpose. This is key to building trust in your community, because you are asking for their most precious resource: time. When you communicate a clear purpose for your meeting, you show your community that you value their time.

MEETING PLANNING TEMPLATE

Purpose:

Date/Time/Location:

Attendees:

Agenda:

- Clarify the reason for the meeting.
- Explore ways to infuse trust and build personal connections among community members, including time for nonwork discussions.
- Take personal responsibility for any recent errors or issues.
- Foster inclusive participation.
- Share responsibility for the agenda, content, and presentations.
- Provide the opportunity for sharing of ideas, insights, feedback, and lessons.
- Include new community members' perspectives.
- Provide opportunities for cross-training among diverse people and functions.
- Encourage creative pairings to build better relationships.
- Create a safe sharing environment.
- Promote experimentation/ask for ideas.

Step Three: Share the Right Data

The overarching purpose of any meeting is to communicate, so most meetings will require you to share information with your community. But this does not mean simply throwing endless bar graphs and pie charts up onto a projector screen and rattling off numbers. The role of the leader is to make sure that data is contextualized and then used to drive decisions and change. Data for data's sake helps no one.

To make sure you share data effectively, start by identifying what data points everyone truly needs to understand to function in your community. These could be quantitative results, such as sales numbers, or they could be qualitative results, such as customer comments. A balance of both is typically most useful.

Once you have selected the data to share, develop your reading of this information. Why is it important? What does it mean in the context of your work? What implications does it have for your community moving forward? Sharing data is an opportunity to reinforce your vision, so be sure to interpret the results in light of your community values and goals.

Turning data points into a story for your community will help everyone understand the facts. It will also provide the reasoning behind your next moves and a touchpoint for judging future results. If you'd like a refresher on honing your storytelling skills as you consider how to share data with your community, refer back to the Story Wave exercise in Session 4.

Step Four: Ask for Participation in Advance

As we discussed in Session 3, inclusivity requires leaders to listen at least as often as they speak. A great meeting is not only a time for you to tell the story of your vision; it's also a time for the community to come together to share opinions and ideas. To foster that interactivity, you must intentionally create space for others to share.

One of the best ways I've found to ensure that community members are engaged in meetings is to ask for feedback in advance. When you send the agenda for the meeting, include a question or two that you wish to discuss. Providing these questions ahead of time gives your community time to preengage with the subject and come prepared to share their thinking. You'll create a shared expectation for the exchange of ideas, and you'll get better, more thoughtful feedback because they've had time to think.

There are, of course, other ways to create an expectation for community participation in your meetings. In fact, I recommend that you shake up your requests for feedback so that you don't fall into a routine—predictability leads to boredom and disengagement! By changing the interactive portions of your meetings around, you'll also model an open, experimental mindset for your community. Instead of saving feedback time for the end, play with the order of your agenda to keep people on their toes. You can begin with the questions you sent in advance or pause in the middle to take questions. You can allow time for pairs or small groups to discuss what they've heard and report back their concerns.

Asking great questions is also key to soliciting feedback. Try adding these to your repertoire:

- What am I missing?

- How could this be streamlined?

- What have we learned?

- Does this make sense to you?

- Do you understand why we are doing this?

- Do you agree?

Step Five: Check Your Mindset

The mood and attitude of the leader greatly influences the whole community, so do a simple check-in with yourself before you begin a meeting. Spend this time thinking about your priorities, reviewing your agenda and any bullet points you've developed to guide your storytelling, and consider repeating your affirmations to help put you in the right frame of mind. Remember, you want to radiate positivity and model open-mindedness.

This mindset check is especially important in video meetings, where you will have to work harder to connect with your community. In addition to your personal qualities, do make sure that your lighting, background, and sound quality are good. Are there ways you can improve your surroundings to better reflect your personality and the overall vibe you want to create? In general, I recommend against using a false backdrop and instead choosing a spot where you feel comfortable and where your team can get a glimpse of your authentic personality.

Presentations Aren't Meetings!

No discussion of meetings would be complete without a discussion of the role of presentations in your communications plan. **Presentations** are informational and used to provide data to your community. They are important, but they're often part of the reason meetings get a bad rap. When presenting information, consider carefully whether the presentation needs to be *synchronous* (delivered in real time) or whether they can be *asynchronous* (recorded for remote workers, presented in an email or PowerPoint ahead of time, etc.).

Meetings, on the other hand, are designed for human-to-human interaction and should provide opportunities for discussion and feedback. Meetings are highly interactive. This distinction is particularly important to remember in a remote environment, where the temptation is great to lean into presentations only. But this is a mistake. To make sure your video conference functions as an effective meeting, you must create opportunities for interaction and discussion, whether by voice, chat, or both. Above all, *cameras must be on* during meetings to facilitate a more human environment where people can gauge reactions and connect to the community as a whole. Rewriting the Story

Let's look back at our story about the CEO who made himself the key figure in his unsustainable schedule of meetings. How could he have designed more effective meetings for his community?

In our work with this company, we stepped in to develop a new meeting strategy. We created a purpose and agenda for a weekly all-hands meeting each Tuesday to bring the entire community together to share information and personal connection. We further consolidated the department meetings into functional alignment meetings, bringing the total from ten down to six—and in the process brought together groups that needed to work more closely with each other. The new cadence of meetings allowed the entire community to come together and share ideas, which allowed them to solve problems and build a thriving culture of collaboration. The leader was no longer a conduit that could make or break connections, but rather the facilitator of human relationships.

Next Steps

New technology has enabled a communication ecosystem that has great potential for creating a more geographically and culturally diverse community. But for a hybrid or remote working environment to be sustainable, leaders must be intentional about finding ways to bring people together. Now more than ever, we need to say yes to meetings.

Well-designed meetings that allow community members to ask questions and provide feedback are central to an effective communication plan. Once you've followed this workflow, you should have the skills to select the right type of meeting for your purpose, design an inclusive and engaging agenda, provide data in context, and make space for your community to come together and share ideas in a safe, supportive environment.

If you'd like additional support in designing your me
agendas, please see the Appendix for additional resources.
can also go to www.notgoingback.net to download meeting
agenda templates for each meeting type to use in your future
planning.

CULTURE
MATTERS

Put It All Together

Throughout the previous six sessions on leadership, we've spoken about transparency, communication, and showing up as a leader. We've largely discussed these skills as personal qualities for individuals to develop to lead a community. But for that community to reach its full potential, all members must embrace those skills for themselves. This is what it means to build a strong culture, and it's especially important in today's highly transparent environment.

In the past, organizations were known primarily by their distinctive products or services. In rarer cases, they might also have made a name for themselves based on operational strengths (think Ford's assembly line or the IBM Way). Even the recent group of technology-driven unicorns have been built with larger-than-life and sometimes flawed individuals at the helm, but the general public had little insight into how these companies operated beyond what they sold.

Then came social media. Suddenly, we have much more insight into exactly how a company's culture operates. We can see how they communicate internally, how they treat their employees, how inclusive they are to diverse workers, and how environmentally sustainable they are. It's not necessarily a whistleblower pulling back the curtain on these issues either. All it takes is a single employee to share some insight in a tweet that goes viral, and suddenly the world takes a much closer look at a company's culture. What was once internal is now all out in the open.

Given this new media environment, communities can no longer keep a dysfunctional culture under wraps. Issues like a company's environmental impact, the ratio of CEO to employee compensation, and the treatment of workers are all critical parts of their operations, and it's all on display. Communities of the future will be held to a much higher standard by the newly empowered public. We are entering an age of community leadership and responsibility that will be out there for all to see.

Are you prepared?

If you have done the work of the previous sessions, you are well on your way toward building a sustainable, transparent culture that will withstand public scrutiny. This isn't a trick of lighting or marketing, however. The only way to thrive in today's high-wattage public spotlight is to make sure that your culture truly reflects your values.

Remember, values are what you stand for; they are the things you believe in. These are things that shouldn't change as the community evolves and grows. In fact, it's what holds it together and attracts new members and customers.

A caveat here: culture is very, very difficult to change after a company is built. To revamp a company culture after many years of entrenchment is like trying to transplant a mature apple tree into better soil. The roots are simply too deep and tangled to make a clean break, and they may not rebound to bear fruit in the future, no matter how carefully you tend to the process. It is much easier to intentionally design a community culture that operates with the right values from the start.

The earlier you take the reins to develop culture as a leader, the stronger your community will be.

A Story: Showing Up

For the final story in this book, I would like to share a personal experience. My first professional opportunity as a leader came early and unexpectedly. I was working as an accessories designer for a startup shoe company. Sometimes the stars align and what you're doing really resonates with the marketplace, and this business took off like a rocket. It was thrilling, gratifying, and maybe even a bit frightening.

I had just turned thirty when I was appointed president and COO. I was now responsible for operating the business and leading the teams during years of extreme growth for the company. This was also a time of extreme inexperience for me personally. I had never been in charge of groups of people before, and I freely admit that I made lots of mistakes.

I am naturally a straightforward person, and the organization trusted me. This was great, but I now know that I didn't do enough to foster a full culture of trust for the community. For example, separate departments and teams were often in conflict, competing against each other for supremacy in the organization rather than cooperating together on cross-functional projects. For example, the wholesale business and the retail stores were never on the same page with each other, which led to conflicts in the overall presentation of our brand: how we looked in our own stores ended up being quite different from how we looked in department stores. If I had been more skilled and intentional about bringing those groups together, the gap between them would not have widened as the business grew.

I also did not fully appreciate the value of diversity or understand the skills of inclusion required to foster it. Our community was diverse in terms of gender and sexual orientation, but not inclusive enough around race. I should have created more opportunities for people of color to enter and thrive in the business.

While the brand was revolutionary in promoting and supporting important social issues, I could have done more to create and define better internal values as the business grew. This would have helped attract a more diverse community, and it would have been incredibly helpful in developing and implementing smart new ideas during a period of rapid growth.

I also must admit that I allowed my personal introversion to keep me from showing up and declaring my values and vision within the organization. I just didn't realize at the time how important it was to communicate vision to the community. If I had been better able to articulate this and model such openness, we could have built a more sustainable and adaptable company from the beginning, when it was still relatively easy to shape the culture in the most fruitful direction.

In the end, I worked hard and was successful in several areas, but I did not yet have the insight or skills to develop a cohesive, sustainable culture.

Culture Workflow

If I had known then what I know now about the role of a leader in creating a sustainable culture, I would have worked from the beginning to make sure that fast-growing organization was a place where diversity was encouraged and ideas flowed freely among all community members. Since that first leadership experience, I have learned a great deal about the skills required to do this, and I present this learning to you here.

This workflow represents the culmination of all of the leadership skills you have developed in the previous sessions. In this workflow, you will take these personal skills public so your community can replicate them in all of their work and interpersonal interactions. In this way, you ensure that your culture at large reflects your personal values as your community grows.

Step One: Model the Behavior

My favorite definition of **culture** is *values in action*. Your community culture is not just a stated philosophy. It is not the mission statement that you drafted and then put in a drawer. Rather, culture is the way you live, work, make decisions, and share your values with others.

Because action is the key to bringing values to life, a leader's first step is to model the behavior you want to see. If you value transparency, make sure your communication cadence and style reflect this. If you value experimentation, be sure to provide opportunities for your community to try new things—and share the results of your own experiments, whether successful or otherwise.

Remember, values are your core principles, and these will not change. The opinions, strategies, and methods that shape your daily work will indeed change to meet the moment, but the values that drive your culture will not. This allows you to adapt to the world while keeping your identity intact.

Understanding this difference will serve as a beacon for your behavior as a leader. Even when storm clouds gather, your values will light the way for the way you and the rest of your community responds.

Step Two: Facilitate Positive Conflict

Many people are surprised to see **conflict** included on a culture creation to-do list. Not all conflict is bad, and a thoughtful clash of ideas is often necessary to move forward—particularly when the world is changing around you.

But this is not to say that conflict requires interpersonal strife or toxic energy to infect your culture. To facilitate positive conflict, you want to allow room for deep questioning and productive disagreements. These kinds of interactions form a solution-oriented process, not a stage for free-floating criticism. Positive conflict means:

- Encouraging questions

- Facilitating disagreements

- Focusing on issues and tasks, not personalities

- Creating a safe space for sharing opinions

- Including alternative views and opinions, particularly from introverts, newcomers, and people of color

If you need some convincing of the power of positive conflict, consider the work of Adam Grant. In his book *Think Again: The Power of Knowing What You Don't Know*, Grant examines over one hundred studies covering eight thousand teams and finds that task conflict (rather than interpersonal conflict) is linked to greater creativity, better choices, and more robust idea generation. He also points out, rightly, that "the absence of conflict is not harmony. It's apathy."[4]

Your community will undoubtedly experience conflict at some point. When you put processes in place that provide a way to productively work through this conflict, you harness the true creative power of your diverse team.

---

4   Adam Grant, *Think Again: The Power of Knowing What You Don't Know* (New York: Viking, 2021).

Step Three: Promote Shared Responsibility and Trust

Transparent communication and personal honesty create trust among your community members. You will model this in your interactions with your partners and role players, of course, but it also makes sense to make shared responsibility structural.

For example, consider basing incentive compensation on group performance rather than individual performance. This is a powerful way of bringing teams together to work toward a goal because everyone works together rather than undermining each other in a competition for limited resources. Likewise, transparency around compensation will go a long way in fostering trust among your community members and limit the backstabbing and "court intrigue" that happens when people are left to guess about the pay scale and raises.

Another important way to foster trust is to lean into weakness. Make asking for help an everyday practice rather than a rare and shameful occurrence. Building a strong mentorship program and providing both formal and informal opportunities to seek advice will help with this. You'll also want to include the whole community in the process of designing your mentorship program so it serves both mentors and mentees well.

Step Four: Honor Risk-Taking and Experimentation

To create a culture that can successfully pivot when circumstances demand it, you'll want to encourage experimentation early on. Think of this as an investment in low-stakes risk-taking now, when things are going well, so that you have already built a practice of experimentation that your community can fall back on when you need to make a quick change in response to future events.

Your goal should be to foster a bias toward decision-making and action. This serves to balance your positive conflict in an important way: no conflict can remain positive for long if it drags on endlessly, so reaching resolutions is key. Discuss the stakes of your decisions openly and present challenges as opportunities. As you come to decisions, prioritize moving forward with concrete actions, making sure that your community members know that these are opportunities to learn and improve. Your members must feel safe to make mistakes, so be sure to discuss the results of experimentation in a spirit of collaboration and learning, not one of discipline and punishment.

Step Five: Use Sustainable Values to Guide Your Culture

This brings us full circle in our discussion of leadership. We began Session 1 with a focus on a sustainable mindset, and now it's time to spread these values outward to your community and beyond. I like to think of sustainable values as impacting three main groups:

- **Individuals:** Developing a culture of clear boundaries between work and life is key. If you haven't done so already, review your work in the area of designing meetings and your choice of communication platforms and norms to protect and honor your community's humanity.

- **Community:** Establish a playbook (see below) that clearly describes the purpose of your community as well as its values and culture. This will serve as a valuable guide for all of your work and will help new community members know how to function at their best in the group.

- **The Planet:** Your community should provide more than individual benefits. Its existence should do something to make the world a better place. Having a higher purpose and making a positive impact on the world are the ties that bind your community together as you work toward a worthy common goal. If you haven't thought about this yet, it's time to do so. Your ability to sustain and grow your community depends on it.

Design Your Community Playbook

Now that you know the steps to follow to build a sustainable culture, it's time to commit. What, exactly, will your culture look like? What purpose and values will drive your work? These are big, important questions that deserve thoughtful answers. To help you organize your thinking, I have developed what I call the Community Playbook. This document will be the go-to guide for your community as you plan new initiatives, interactions, and decisions.

You can, of course, begin brainstorming elements of your Community Playbook on your own. But keep in mind that you cannot dictate culture from on high. You'll need to include your partners and role players in this collaborative work as well.

THE COMMUNITY PLAYBOOK

OUR PURPOSE
Why does your community exist?

OUR CULTURE
What is your vision for your culture?

Elements of Our Culture
What strategies will you employ to make sure each element of your culture reflects your values and supports your community?

Brand:	Diversity, Equity, and Inclusion:

Compensation:	Hiring:

Communication:	Work-Life Boundaries:

Environmental Impact:	Experimentation:

OUR VALUES
Who are you, and what unshakable values will guide your community through change over time?

The Community Playbook takes serious reflection to complete, but the results are well worth the effort to provide a living document that you can refer to as you build a sustainable community for the future.

Rewriting the Story

In real life, we don't always get to go back and right the wrongs or change the endings of our stories. If I could do things over, I would have used the Community Playbook I shared above to build a culture of greater collaboration and inclusion, and I believe this would have solved many of the problems that ended up being baked into that shoe company as it grew. The company still exists today and continues to do excellent work supporting social issues. But it has shrunk in recent years, due in large part to the divisions among its different elements. Over time, the lack of communication became an uncrossable chasm.

As for me, I spent the rest of my career after that working to become a more collaborative and inclusive CEO. I worked with focused intentionality to learn from those early experiences and develop my leadership skills, and I'm constantly honing and adapting those skills to the changing world.

The result of that learning is what I present here to you: a clear guide for fostering a sustainable culture that will help your community thrive.

I didn't have the tools or the guidance to know where to begin.

Now you do.

Conclusion

H ave you heard of CEO Disease?
It's an ironic byproduct of success. This condition creeps up on leaders who have been at the helm of an organization for so long that they become like a king who never leaves the throne room. This leader has surrounded himself with smart people who do whatever he says, so he no longer has to get creative to solve problems. His skills get a little dull, and it doesn't help that he's gotten very used to hearing the word "yes."

When a leader succumbs to CEO Disease, he begins to think he's always right because he is never challenged. Though he feels strong, this leader has actually been weakened by his disconnection from his partners and role players, and all it takes is one unexpected challenge to reveal how unprepared he is to respond.

Now more than ever, leaders are grappling with how best to stay engaged with their work and their communities. How do you keep learning and find ways to roll with the many changes that are happening all around you?

I've spent my career fighting against CEO Disease, and this book represents my best effort at preventive medicine.

If you've read through all of the sessions, you've engaged in a two-part process. First, you've begun to develop the mindset and skills you need to lead. These come from within, and the work is deeply personal. Second, you've begun to make the shift from student to teacher, in that you are learning to engender that same mindset and skillset in your community at large. This is what will keep you fresh and agile for the long haul.

I would like to note here that it is the work itself that keeps you fresh. Leadership is a process—one that you're never really finished with. In each of these sessions, you've worked to answer some important questions. At this point in your journey, my hope is that you've developed some answers to each of them:

- Why is self-awareness so important, and how can you achieve it?

- How can you intentionally design your culture?

- How do you develop a more inclusive community?

- How can your organization adapt to change while staying focused on its mission?

- How can we sustain ourselves, our community, and our planet as we grow?

Only you can answer these questions, and your answers will be unique to you, your values, and your mission. Your answers will also change over time. This is necessary and right. To stay fresh and focused as a leader, you will need to revisit your thinking and adjust as your community grows and the world around you changes. That is the work of leadership: constantly checking in to ensure that you evolve in ways that are true to your values.

My hope is that this book serves as your guide in this work. You can begin with the session that means the most to you— whether it solves your most immediate problem or helps you grow in an exciting new direction. Once you've read it and discussed it and thought about it, it's time to do something.

So take a step. Make it happen. Begin this meaningful work. It will prepare you for the changes that will be coming in the world. We cannot predict those changes, but we do know that the future will look nothing like the past. By preparing yourself and your community with strong values and a flexible mind-set now, you'll be prepared for anything. You will be a better leader, and your people will be happier. They'll live a more fulfilled life, and that, in turn, will improve the entire planet.

The time to start is now, because we're not going back.

And with such incredible power to be a force for positive change, why would you want to?

Appendix

One of the keys to being an effective leader is to adopt the stance of a lifelong learner. Here are additional books and resources that have informed my thinking and that I recommend to you as you continue your development.

For Further Reading

The Good Jobs Strategy: How the Smartest Companies Invest in Employees to Lower Costs and Boost Profits
Zeynep Ton
New Harvest, 2014

In-depth case studies that prove smart investments in happy and motivated employees can actually save organizations money and help them do better work.

Think Again: The Power of Knowing What You Don't Know
Adam Grant
Viking, 2021

Research-based studies and storytelling about the importance of self-awareness and adaptability.

Mindset: The New Psychology of Success
Carol S. Dweck
Ballantine Books, 2007

Research-based work that focuses on how we think about ourselves—and how that affects performance and accomplishment.

Primal Leadership: Unleashing the Power of Emotional Intelligence
Daniel Goleman, Richard Boyatzis, and Annie McKee
Harvard Business Review Press, 2013

A classic work that shows the importance of emotional intelligence and the effect of resonant leaders on group performance.

The Inclusive Mindset: How to Cultivate Diversity in Your Everyday Life
Justin Jones-Fosu
Peter Jones Publishing, 2021

Practical examples and helpful strategies to make inclusivity a stronger habit.

The Practice of Adaptive Leadership: Tools and Tactics for Changing Your Organization and the World
Ronald Heifetz
Harvard Business Press, 2009

In-depth study of techniques and examples of adaptive leadership in environments of extreme change.

Group Genius: The Creative Power of Collaboration
Keith Sawyer
Basic Books, 2017

Clearly outlines the benefits and results of collaboration in the creative process.

Restoring the Soul of Business: Staying Human in the Age of Data
Rishad Tobaccowala
Harper Collins Leadership, 2020

An inspiring philosophical work describing the fusion of technology, data, and humanity.

Personal Resources
Amy Jin
www.AmyJin.com
Leadership coaching based in the practice of mindfulness.

Mitchell Nash
www.MomentLeadership.com
Change-management leadership coaching.

Rob Smith
www.ThePhluidProject.com
Gender-expansive training and coaching.

Justin Jones-Fosu
www.WorkMeaningful.com
Inclusivity coaching, training, and consulting.

Acknowledgments

I'd like to start by thanking my children. You are a window for me to see how fast the world is changing and are constantly reminding me of how much I have to learn.

To all of the people I've worked with and had the honor to lead for the past thirty years: you've inspired me to learn and grow with you, and that has been an amazing and exciting journey.

I'd also like to thank my partners at The Ember Company for their constant encouragement and support while some of my time and attention were given to this book.

Special thanks for inspiration and input on challenging sections from Seth Godin, Susan Brecker, David Billstrom, Justin Jones-Fosu, Mitchell Nash, Jack Anderson, and Joshua Blum.

This book never would have happened without the incredible team at Lioncrest Publishing: Mikey Kershisnek, Vi La Bianca, Brannan Siratt, Erik van Mechelen, and finally, my amazing Scribe, teacher, and guide, Elizabeth Trach.

About the Author

Paul Blum has applied his strategic vision to iconic brands for more than thirty years. In addition to his role as Executive Chairman of The Ember Company, Paul serves as an advisor and board director to several companies. He previously served as CEO of several global luxury and fashion retail firms, including Kenneth Cole Productions, David Yurman, Fred Segal, Juicy Couture, and Henri Bendel. A self-described "permanent student," Paul deeply immerses himself in the details to bring each moving part together into a cohesive whole. Paul is also a committed teacher who has mentored founders and consults with both small and large business clients to build viable strategies for the future.

Paul spends his free time skiing, hiking, and mountain biking. He's recently developed a regular yoga practice as well. He and his wife work together on the Blum Family Fund, which focuses on organizations benefiting global literacy and less privileged youth.